Praise for *The Book of (More) Delights*

Named a Best Book of the Year by the
Boston Globe, Garden & Gun, Electric Literature,
and St. Louis Public Radio

Named a Most-Anticipated Book by *Time,*
Kirkus Reviews, Publishers Weekly, Book Riot,
and the *Christian Science Monitor*

"This tour of delights is itself a delight." —*The Boston Globe*

"Keenly observed and delivered with deftness, these essays are a testament to the artfulness of attention and everyday joy."

—*Kirkus Reviews*

"Ross Gay follows up his 2019 bestseller, *The Book of Delights*, with another collection of charming essays as quirky, engaging, and wryly humorous as the first."

—*The Christian Science Monitor*

"Another startling, sensuous collection of miniature essays . . . Again and again, joy wins out over despair as Gay pays tribute to a world of people 'bumbling, flailing, hurting, failing, [and] changing.'"

—*Booklist*

"Ross Gay, and I will praise him forever, is a beautiful writer who reminds us of the beauty in small, everyday things."

—Ann Patchett, *The Skimm*

"Enchanting . . . These unforgettable vignettes will enhance readers' appreciation for their own surroundings."

—*Publishers Weekly*

"Short essays with wonderfully playful writing that made me feel understood while also providing a new way to see the world . . . Somet[illegible] you need a quick pick-me-up[illegible]

[illegible]. Louis Public Radio

"A feel-good book . . . The book's happy, worry-free vibes make it the ultimate vacation read, no matter the time of year."

—*Travel + Leisure*

"Gay proves that he's able to endlessly expand on any minute detail of life in a way that's not only interesting, but that's often profound, open-ended, and sometimes even revelatory. It's clear that these 'delights' are a gift not only for the author himself but also for every one of the readers he touches." —Shondaland

"Yes, please, I'll have another dose of delight."

—Margaret Roach, *The New York Times*

"Enormously delightful." —*Literary Hub*

"Ross Gay's 'delight practice' turns out to be exactly what I need to cope with this whole being-a-human-in-2024 thing . . . A gloriously unpredictable compendium of observations and celebrations of a life lived with full attention."

—*The Guardian* (US)

"By popular demand, Ross Gay is back, better than ever . . . This time he swings his basket higher, slower, for a whole new bevy of brainy and witty noticings." —*Garden & Gun*

"[Gay] calls on us to marvel at nature's small wonders and remember that we're all connected." —*The Washington Post*

"Gay's prose is like a symphony . . . Prepare to be enchanted, uplifted, and ultimately transformed." —Medium

"Heartening. Informal yet inspired, off-the-cuff yet beautifully composed . . . *The Book of (More) Delights* provides abundant avenues to appreciate our world." —BookPage

"Gay's work never sugarcoats the difficulties or fragility of life, but it is still so hopeful." —*USA Today*

The Book of *(More)* Delights

Ross Gay

ALGONQUIN BOOKS OF CHAPEL HILL 2024

Published by
ALGONQUIN BOOKS OF CHAPEL HILL
an imprint of Workman Publishing
a division of Hachette Book Group, Inc.
1290 Avenue of the Americas
New York, NY 10104

First paperback edition, Algonquin Books of Chapel Hill, October 2024. Originally published in hardcover by Algonquin Books of Chapel Hill in September 2023.

Excerpt from "Hammond B Organ Cistern"
by Gabrielle Calvocoressi, courtesy of Persea Books.

Printed in the United States of America.
Design by Steve Godwin.

Library of Congress Cataloging-in-Publication Data
Names: Gay, Ross, [date]– author.
Title: The book of (more) delights / Ross Gay.
Description: Chapel Hill, North Carolina : Algonquin Books of Chapel Hill, [2023] | Includes bibliographical references. | Summary: "A collection of essays in which the author discusses the small and large things that delight him"—Provided by publisher.
Identifiers: LCCN 2023015049 | ISBN 9781643753096 (hardcover) | ISBN 9781643755472 (ebook)
Subjects: LCSH: Gay, Ross, [date]—Anecdotes. | Joy—Anecdotes. | LCGFT: Essays.
Classification: LCC PS3607.A9857 B66 2023 | DDC 814/.6—dc23/eng/20230428
LC record available at https://lccn.loc.gov/2023015049

ISBN 978-1-64375-635-6 (paperback)

10 9 8 7 6 5 4 3 2 1

First Paperback Edition

Contents

ALSO BY ROSS GAY

Inciting Joy

Be Holding

The Book of Delights

Catalog of Unabashed Gratitude

Bringing the Shovel Down

Against Which

Introduction

WHEN I WRAPPED up the first *Book of Delights*, August 1 of 2017, I was at a writing residency in Marfa, Texas, with my friend Patrick Rosal. We swung some kettlebells, shot some hoops, ate the birthday lentils he cooked me, and somewhere in there, after congratulating me on finishing the book, he asked me if I was going to keep writing delights. It hadn't occurred to me before he said it. I had been thinking of the book as a kind of one-off. Besides, I had other projects I was working on, and excited to get to. At the same time, the yearlong project I had just completed felt like it would be a useful, fun, and unpredictable *lifelong* project, so I eventually decided every five years would be right. I started this one on August 1, 2021.

I kept to the same constraints—write them daily, write them quickly, and write them by hand—though truth be told, I was a little looser with those this time around, for one of the delights of a constraint, or a rule, is breaking it. If you read the first *Delights*, much will be familiar: Bloomington, Indiana, where I live and teach. The garden my partner, Stephanie, and I tend and are tended by. Lots of beloved friends. More considerations of public space. More (hard to believe!) coffee shops. More interactions with strangers. More questions about power and authority. More books and music. More of my dear mother, who, as the days go on, has become one of the foremost prompts of my delight. And though some of the specific characteristics of the tumult during which this book was written might seem novel, the tumult, the trouble, the confusion, the rage, and the sorrow, I suspect, will not.

But what feels like a discovery—I mean, I had a hunch from the first book, but now it's bloomed from hunch into understanding—has been given to me over these last couple years in conversations with readers who tell me they have taken up their own delight (or some ancillary *noticing-and-paying-attention-to-and-thinking-about-what-you-love*) practice. Quite a few of these people tell me that they do their delight practice with other people—a morning phone call of delights; a zoom delights group; a delight pen pal; a weekly amble of delights with a friend through the neighborhood. And several of these people have told me that their practice has inspired other people to do their own practices. As they thank me, sometimes suggesting I'm the origin point of their delight practice, I try to remember to point out to them that my delight practice, my *delights*, were likewise given to me. Whether it's the bird who told me to write the first *Delights*, or the essays I was reading as I wrote them, or Patrick wondering if I'd write another one, or the people who gave me a beautiful notebook or helped me in the laundromat or hugged me in the co-op (or the news of all these delights groups), they've all been given to me; they've all been given to *us*. And they become more given, and more *received*, upon being shared. (See Robin Wall Kimmerer; See Lewis Hyde.) Which, quiet as it's kept,[1] we seem inclined to do: share

---

1 And believe me: it's kept quiet. Because disbelieving in care, in sharing, in the everyday banal precious luminous potential and in-our-face goodness of each other; disbelief, too, in the fact that we are so often the source of, the tether to, each other's delight: i.e., *when we disbelieve in each other*, we are an easy mark; we are a market. I am grateful to whoever it was pointed out to me how in the airport every few minutes we're reminded by a voice that I assume is meant to be neutral and beneficent and caring descending to us from invisible loudspeakers not to leave our bags unattended because someone might slip in a bomb that they got through the X-ray machines, I guess? It's one of a thousand often subtle examples of the concerted effort to keep us on the lookout *against* each other, to erode our faith in one another,

what delights us; share what we love. For the record, before you go there, I'm not being optimistic. I'm just paying attention.

And finally: this time around, a sucker for appendixes and gratitude (or appendixes of gratitude), I have included a list of some of the books I was reading and learning from and *learning how* from while writing and revising these essayettes. Additionally, because the older I get the harder time I have dispensing with my delights, I've included an abridged assemblage of some of the delights whose full form for whatever reason (page count; redundancy of theme; not a good essay) did not make it into the book.

I'm pretty sure so that we will give that faith, which kinda has to go somewhere, to the invisible voice in the sky, which, given how sick and broke and homeless and poisoned and uninsured and overworked and hurting and lonely so many of us seem to be, well, I don't know if whatever that voice belongs to actually cares about us. But I firmly believe you do. And I firmly believe *we* do. The evidence is everywhere. And that care—mutual, radiant, unpredictable, sloppy, mycelial, transgressive—seems to be what *The Delights* are on the lookout for.

1. My Birthday, Again

WELL, HERE WE are again: this time, my forty-seventh birthday. This year we decided to enjoy a week away up in a little rented cabin in Vermont, which has a bounty of delights. The first of which is that apple trees grow everywhere here—yards, roadside thickets, parking lots—and this year they're loaded. I mean I have never seen forageable bounty quite like this, and it makes me want to come back with a pickup truck to snag a few years' worth of applesauce. As we were driving around, admiring all the apple trees, I was also admiring that very Vermonty and Catholic-sounding roadside feature called the pull-out. Also called pull-offs, they are common here as air, room enough for a few cars to pull over and look down at the beautiful river roiling though the boulders below, or overlook the valley with the first embers of fall in the leaves. Shortly after we pulled out of a pull-off, we pulled into yet another of the delights of Vermont, a roadside farm stand, this one peopled by people, though sometimes they're peopled solely by a box in which to slide your money. A trust-box I've never heard it called, though we should. As we were getting some blueberries and raspberries, we overheard some Vermontahs who were happily whooped from summiting a pass earlier today. They described it while picking out their fruit—"beautiful" this and "beautiful" that; challenging but fun—so we got directions from them, and after we settled up, we headed there.

The trail started right at the edge of the parking lot, which was more like a pull-off, and we entered what was immediately a lush and magical forest: birches with their bark curling like pages of old books; ferns luminous from the light dappling through the canopy; plush carpets of moss; nearly fluorescent mushrooms. It was ruggedish, lots of scrambling up slick slabs of, I think, granite. We were both sweating pretty good within the first half hour or so, and Stephanie stashed her sweatshirt behind a fallen tree. We passed through what felt like several ecosystems, and when, about two hours later, we finally approached a sign that we knew in our heart of hearts was going to tell us a hundred feet, maybe fifty, to the summit, it said one mile to go.

We'd only eaten a couple handfuls of berries, I'd only brought a not-all-the-way-full quart glass jar of water for both of us, and as we were contemplating reaching the top, a couple hikers approached the same sign we were looking at.

They both had on big packs; one looked to be about mid-sixties, the other late twenties or early thirties. We learned they worked together and were practicing for a longer trip on the Appalachian Trail, with which this trail intersected. The older of the two was the boss, she had hiking poles, and the younger looked a little bit coerced. The boss asked us which way we were going, and we told her that we were deciding whether or not to go the final mile, pointing in the direction of the summit. Upon which she looked us up and down, noting I guess our attire, T-shirts and shorts, and asked us, or maybe actually she was telling us: *You know cotton's a killer, right?* Then pointing to our feet (unsupportive sneakers) she made an *Are you kidding me?* face and shook her head no. Then she asked how much water we had, and I shook the half-full quart glass jar, cutely I thought, at which she sneered *That's not even close to enough*—making an "Are you stupid?" face—*and no glass on the trail!* I was already backing away, trying to sneak down the trail, for who wants to get chewed out on their birthday, when Stephanie for some reason blabbed about *Yeah, I'm a little hungry* and *Yeah, I have a little bit of a headache* and *Yeah, my knee's kind of bothering me, too*, blah blah, at which I recoiled and ducked my head, like *Why would you tell her that*, like *She's going to yell at me*, which, in a Vermontah way she did. In full-on take-your-head-out-of-your-ass-ese, she asked, I mean she actually asked, *What's wrong with you?* After we told her *everything is wrong with us you're right thank you so much and no more glass on the trail sorry about that ma'am* she said, sort of chipper again, *Okay, take care now! Enjoy Vermont!* As we were descending, we could hear her talking shit about us to the ranger a few yards farther up the trail, *She was hungry! He had a glass jar! They were wearing cotton!*

Trotting down, enjoying myself, trying to not smoke Stephanie and her hurting knee and head, I found myself whistling and feeling the soft earth receiving my inadequate footwear, and the glowing ferns dragging their feathery fronds along my suicidal cotton shorts. And I noted how pleased I was, delighted even, as I tend often to be, at having not reached the summit. To have gotten close but no cigar. An interesting quality I was turning over in my head on my glad descent. Maybe I'm afraid of failure? Maybe I'm afraid of the ends of things? Maybe it's a rejection of the conquering spirit of some of my forefathers? Maybe it's a distant cousin to the way

I for some reason always leave out a tiny bit of a few ingredients when I'm cooking—a few slices of onion, a couple very small potatoes, three florets of broccoli or cauliflower? Maybe it's a small and weird gesture of hope, leaving something in the tank for tomorrow, which implies there will be a tomorrow? Maybe not finishing is a prayer for the tomorrow?

An interesting prayer to make on the first day of a yearlong project. Though it was a dueling prayer I made when Stephanie brought home four very delicious birthday tacos for me, which, along with the chips and guac, and the kimchi, and the roasted sweet potatoes, and the kombucha, I did in fact summit.

(Aug. 1)

2. The Wide Berth

TODAY, AS I walked on a narrow-shouldered road, very distracted by the abundance of forageable food—more rogue apples, raspberries, chokecherries, a whole eight-foot wall of thimble berries; it's like Willy Wonka's out here!—these Vermontahs driving in their Subarus or pickups almost to a one gave me a wide berth, veering a good eight or so feet away from me. Sometimes they crossed all the way across the double line into the other lane. And most often, while berthing me widely, they waved.

Though this is not the first berth of note, of delight, for today is my beloved friend Walt's fiftieth birthday. No doubt some extra confetti for this party because Walt was supposed to be a goner, from leukemia, over a decade ago, not to mention that, like me, he's had an intermittently troubled mind, he's had a mind itself intermittently difficult to survive, and yet here he is, here we are, still together on this side, our friendship nearly forty years old, which some days makes me look at it like it's my child, I guess it's our child, to say, *My god, you're forty years old. How'd that happen?*

Our forty-year-old child, which we have watched grow up, which we have grown up together, is one of the great comforts of my life. All that becoming, all that floundering, all that stumbling, all that wonder. Walt's the one helped me with my slap shot. Walt's the one told me how to cook eggs. Walt's the one helped me paint the shirt I donned at homecoming that said FUCK APARTHEID on the front and STOP POLICE BRUTALITY on the back. Walt's the one picked me up when I needed a ride, gave me money when I needed it, shared his sorbet, his gummy bears, his cheesesteak and pizza, his extra hockey stick, his car. Walt's the one who said, when I was not quite sure how to extract myself from a relationship that was making me sad, *Dude, what are you doing?* Walt's the one who would tell me I'm fucking up but would never judge me a fuck-up. Walt's the one who makes me think of Donny Hathaway's "He Ain't Heavy, He's My Brother." Walt's the one who never fled from my need, flailing and sloppy and shitty and even cruel sometimes though it might be, which maybe explains why I will never put his phone number in my phone; I keep it by (my) heart.

Oh, one last thing; sort of a first thing, truth be told. For my seventeenth birthday, when I still mainly only read the sports page of the *Bucks County Courier Times*, dude gave me Kant's *Critique of Pure Reason* and Nietzsche's *Beyond Good and Evil.* Which you might call, in addition to throwing your money down the drain, setting a ridiculously high bar. Or you might call it *belief,* which, though I never would have said this out loud, I have actually needed people to have in me. I have needed to be—we need to be—believed in. Which, in a certain kind of way, is like being birthed. And just like his gummy bears and hockey sticks, I guess I'm taking Walt's birthday. Because when Walt was born, so too was I.

(Aug. 3)

3. Jeff Being Jeff

WE VISITED OUR friends Jeff and Colleen today, taking a nice long walk together on a rail-to-trail path a few towns over, before Stephanie and I picked up some Nepalese food to take back to the house. After we'd unpacked the food and carefully dished it up, sitting at the table on their porch overlooking the ravine, Jeff asked if anyone had been fired as fast as he had. Though Colleen and I had both quit jobs on our first days, and we'd all been fired, Jeff took the cake, as he knew he would, by telling us he was canned after a couple of hours working in a bakery in Los Angeles because he couldn't stop sneezing, often in the flour, which, he explained, is why every Angeleno born after that day has a little bit of his DNA. (Popular bakery, I guess.) On his way out he asked the boss if he could at least have a free bag of cookies. Chocolate-chip walnut, preferably. Sadly, he was rebuffed.

Because Jeff was on a roll talking about his numerous shitty jobs, all of which are the source of numerous good stories, he told us about his year or so stacking pipe on an assembly line at Minneapolis Welding Rod during his twenties. Jeff being Jeff, he quickly learned the geriatric machine was finicky and prone to jamming. A quick study and hard worker in the admirable pursuit of laziness—dude actually taught a poetry class in which the students were instructed, during class, to take a nap—he figured out that the machine could be encouraged to jam by feeding a pipe the slightest bit wrong, or right, depending on your perspective, which would make the machine screech to a halt. When the engineers would bring their toolboxes to fix the jam, Jeff would hem and haw, *This damn machine* and such, *Goddamn this piece of shit* and such, before finding a quiet corner where he could stretch out, pull out his paperback, and I guarantee sometimes take a little nap.

(Aug. 4)

4. Communal Walking Stick

TODAY IN VERMONT, meandering without purpose or GPS or map, headed nowhere and on no clock and anticipating nothing, getting lost I guess I'm saying—to an extent; we were in a car with a mostly full tank—which always makes me think of Rebecca Solnit's book *A Field Guide to Getting Lost,* somewhere at the top of my list of most important books evidenced not only by how many times I've read it, but by how many copies I've had and, well, lost. In our lostness—Stephanie and I are in the (god willing) middle of our lives, so let me invoke a little Dante, too:

> Midway upon the journey of our life
> I found myself within a forest dark,
> For the straightforward pathway had been lost.

. . . a little grandiose but still kinda true—we saw a little sign tucked into the branches of a tree like an owl, pointing in the direction of a town woods. First of all, nice concept, a town woods. Second of all, we followed the sign as far as the road took us, dead-ending in a pull-off-ish parking lot, at which point, just ahead of us, the woods, a forest dark, began. There was a meandering trail, a chatty stream cascading periodically over waterfalls that seemed almost to cut terraces into the land. More birches, this time some more maples, and ferns again growing from all the fragrant leaf litter and moss turning into soil on the boulders.

After a couple hours of wandering, and lots of meandering, not quite lost (but neither were we found), we headed back toward the car, thanking the woods as we left, which took the form, mostly, of running our hands along most everything we could reach. Stephanie wanted a few minutes alone by the side of the creek, so I kept following the trail back to the parking lot, at the beginning of which, leaning against a birch tree, was a perfect walking stick. I picked it up: sturdy, straight enough, not too heavy, a good height I bet for most people. And lying at that stick's feet I saw a few others, a little stouter or crookeder, not quite as perfect, though perfect's a dumb idea, don't you think? I had stumbled upon a way station for walking sticks, or better yet, a walking-stick lending library. *Oh, this is a thing*, I realized. *This is something we do.*

(Aug. 5)

5. The Perfect Notebook

OR MAYBE NOT perfect but perfect enough, though I could write an entire manifesto on the perfect notebook, for which I have been searching my whole life it seems like, sometimes in a kind of fugue state in the notebook store (they sell other stuff, but I don't care; well, that's not true: pens, too) in Manhattan on Eighth Street between Fifth and Sixth, or in Meg's beautiful store in Frenchtown,[1] caressing the leaves of every bound thing

---

1 Worth noting that the best notebooks are sometimes gifts, and are probably endowed with some magic on account of being so: the packet of three from Hong Kong with butterflies on the manila-colored cover; the big unlikely sketchbook that was a birthday present; a Moleskine or Field Notes pocket-sized notebook shared from someone else's packet of three; or the beautiful Japanese notebooks I gave to Stephanie for Christmas, which she gifted back because I begged her they were so beautiful; the small hardback journal with a humanoid in a backbend on the cover that I picked up at Meg's store, and when I handed it to her to initiate the transaction,

while looking into space trying to discern through the ears on my fingertips if this one or this one or this one or this one is going to draw from my pen what brilliance is hiding deep somewhere in there, whispering or percolating or murmuring—look, to deny the mysticality of the process is a crock, I mean seriously, I actually think sometimes it's the notebook (or more precisely the soiree between the notebook and pen; the tooth of the paper and the viscosity of the ink, let alone the inherent spiritual endowments of each) that—*who*—makes the poem, the essay, the dream, come forth on the page *on account of the page*, you see what I'm saying, it's a lot of pressure to put on a notebook; I'm thinking today about the notebook I'm writing these delights in, whose paper is a touch too slick (lacking tooth) and whose dimensions a bit too large (lacking pocketability) and rules a bit too square (it's graph paper) because it's actually a gradebook—or better yet, a GRADEBOOK, as it says in red ink—stolen from my place of employ, which I think I will continue to do for this whole year, *liberate* is the better word, swords into ploughshares as it is, which, too, a notebook might whisper to us, or draw from us, so the least we can do is listen, even if imperfectly so.

(Aug. 8)

---

she handed it back to me and said, *It's yours. I hope it gives you some words*. Of course it did.

6. The Perfect Spoon (or Cup)

BUT NOT ONLY notebooks, I'm realizing today, rifling through the spoon drawer past several serviceable spoons (we are not spoon poor), looking for one of our three truly beautiful spoons. Today's spoon is hardy, dense yet elegant, and with a slight impression—as though touched by an angel—on the handle. The bowl of the spoon is just deep enough, and neither too circular nor too pointy. Often when I lift it from the drawer I will balance it on my finger, I'm not sure why. But I know this spoon—the way it looks, the way it was made—makes everything taste better. It is the same for me with bowls (when it comes to the oatmeal I'm eating, I will only eat from one of two bowls), and for coffee I usually drink from the one with the frogs on it (not for the frogs; for the shape, how it fits in my hand

and feels against my mouth; the frogs, though, are an obvious bonus).

I attribute my particular brand of object adoration—certain discrete objects; not in sets, *never* in sets—not solely but largely to Cootie (government name, Scott), an architect and designer with whom I grew up, and from whom I learned, often very soon after he had learned, what makes beautiful human-made objects beautiful. He taught me the concept of "lines" and such. And that a bowl or pair of sunglasses or watch or car might have good ones. It was he who pointed out that a chair might be both comfortable (which before Cootie would have been my sole measure) *and* beautiful, or a sofa, or the table where you eat your oatmeal, or the bedside table on which you place not only your coffee cup, but your bowl of oatmeal, or, the especially transgressive among you, your popcorn.

The summer after Scott and I graduated from college, after we had already traveled to the Salk Institute in La Jolla and the Modern Art Museum of Fort Worth, and after we had studied inside and out Louis Kahn's poetic lectures compiled in the book *What Will Be Always Has Been*—one of the books I studied most closely as I was starting to write poems—Scott and I pilgrimaged to almost all of Louis Kahn's buildings in the Northeast. A science building at the University of

Pennsylvania, some dorms at Bryn Mawr, a housing project in West Philly, the Esherick House just outside of Philadelphia, the Yale University Art Gallery, and the Phillips Exeter Academy Library up in New Hampshire. There are photos out there somewhere (ominous phrase) of that last trip. Close-ups of the poured concrete walls. The famous interior. And one of me vomiting next to the library, painting one of those walls with a pinkish streak of upchuck, which Cootie and I, boys of a certain age, thought was pretty fun, although the puke was the chunky evidence of an ongoing mostly unspoken and completely unspeakable difficult time during which the awful human-made, or the human-made awful, was really rattling around in my mind like a maraca. I guess my head was the maraca, and the awful was what filled it up.

No small balm in the midst of which to have a friend pointing out, too, what is not only un-awful, but truly beautiful, the truly beautiful human-made, the human made beautiful, and how it might catch the light or gather us in or feel in our hands or hold what we're carrying. To have a friend in the midst hold a spoon up to you, and then hand it over, as a way of letting you know, *but also this.*

(Aug. 9)

7. The Clothesline

THERE ARE SO many simple pleasures, simple delights, and maybe the goal, the practice, is to be delighted especially by them, the simplest of things. For instance, today, among the many, I offer the clothesline, not only for its utility, how it keeps the house from getting hot in the summer, how it saves a little energy and burns a little less CO_2, but also for how it reminds you that your grandma in northern Minnesota loved to hang her sheets on a clothesline in the winter for how they smelled after they froze, and that your mother loves the smell of anything hung out. But also this, I'm thinking today, as I admire my T-shirts and shorts and drawers and towels blowing in the wind like Tibetan flags, like a ramshackle and sometimes threadbare rainbow: that a clothesline reminds you how often we make of our simple daily labors (hanging clothes, folding clothes, washing dishes, arranging the fridge or the cupboards, chopping veggies or wrapping the bread, sweeping up, or mopping) an art.

(Aug. 11)

8. Free Stuff

THIS PAST WEEK there has been a pile of stuff on a table on Fourth Street with the sign FREE STUFF. The pile changes a little each day—today, in addition to the clothes, towels, and box of knick-knacks, there is a pile of dishes—which makes me think they're gradually cleaning out. Lightening their load. Each time I cruise by this FREE STUFF table I find myself delighted, I guess because it is yet more evidence of our impulse to share, even if the stuff is, to invoke George Carlin, shit. Because just as one person's stuff is another's shit, one person's shit is another person's stuff.

When my older brother and I were kids, our mother would sometimes get us clothes at yard sales, where the not-quite-free shit was to us sometimes really nice stuff. I can remember one sale on a corner lot in Levittown where my brother and I both got a couple nice shirts, though my brother scored hardest because his was a three-quarter-sleeved jersey, all red, with the letters TG iron-on'd to the left shoulder. *Tough Guy*, he probably thought, which would help him when that bully Kevin tried to stick his face in the mud next time. When he next was racing Nicole Gervazio. This was the kind of shirt that could make you win.

Though my brother was a smart little guy, kind of the smartest little guy in the neighborhood—he aced the Iowa tests and the spelling tests and the vocab tests and he spent an hour or two a week in the academically talented (A.T.) classroom, and it might even be argued that most of his eight thousand fights (the most boring fights in the history of fights) and his many pairs of broken glasses (about which my parents actually seriously considered taking him to a child psychologist, although to my folks that would have been like sending him to the moon) were provoked by his being a smart-little-guy-cum-a-smart-*assed* little guy, you know the face those smart-asses can make when you don't know how to write your name yet, when you can't get it through your thick head that 12 x 12=144—he somehow missed that the Tough Guy acronym on his shoulder could also be, as some everyday dimwit bully in the apartments did not, "The Gay." Which, in 1982 Levittown, bastion of bigotry (and strip malls), was not a compliment.

Around this same time—ages seven and nine, say, respectively—my brother and I used to take a blanket to the front of the apartments, or sometimes a card table, on which we would station and sell our stuff, stuff that had become I guess our shit, and which probably, definitely, belonged on a free stuff table. *What sellable goods does a seven-year-old have?*, you're asking. Good question. Maybe a couple crinkly comic books? A matchbox car? A shirt they've outgrown, maybe a red jersey with the initials TG on the shoulder? I can't remember if we made Jell-O squares or lemonade, though I know you couldn't pay me to eat something a child, especially a group of them, especially boys, was selling. Whatever we were hocking, hand to god, people pulled over on the often busy Trenton Road to inspect, and not infrequently buy, our shit. Sometimes Joey and Mikey or Maurice would join us, none of whom, for the record, had better stuff than we. Their stuff was shit, though shit we'd think was stuff, as was ours to them, so we'd sometimes trade before opening the doors to our card table.

When the adults pulled over and walked up onto the grass, they looked over our shit, we looked over their looking-over, answered any questions they might have about whether or not the toy still worked, was it fixable. Etc. Sometimes we got into provenance and such.

Sometimes the adults, who were really big to us, like giants in Buicks and Pintos and stuff, would want to negotiate. They would try to talk us down. I can't quite imagine having great bargaining skills at that age, in part because I was seven, and in part because I was quite shy. But we did our best. If they tried to low-ball us too hard, we told them they could take their business to some other card table peopled by children.

By the end of our workday we almost always sold enough shit to go to the bar, which was Wheeler's penny candy store, down the hill. It was called a penny candy store, I'm pretty sure, because you could get candy for a penny. Which means a quarter made you flush. A very old man (he was probably about sixty) named Wheeler owned it, he wore suspenders, there was a bell on the door, and he put the candy—Swedish Fish, Rolos, Smarties, Mike & Ikes—in petite paper bags for us as we pulled coins from our sneakers, or, if it was a good day, bills from socks. We walked home sometimes on the side of Trenton Road, and sometimes through the trails, a little gang of entrepreneurial urchins with their hard-earned sacks of candy, never even heard of a water bottle, as free, you might say, as we'd ever be.

(Aug. 15)

9. Daisy Returns

THE CAT WE cohabitate with, common parlance "our cat," though it's obvious enough that we belong to her, is sitting atop my legs, which are beneath a hand-made, old-timey quilt, liver-spotted with coffee stains as bed-clothes in my proximity always are and probably always will be. You are who you are, I once told my friend Sebastian when he got eggs on his shirt again. Daisy takes off on the regular because there have been dogs and another cat who intermittently visit or live here. One of those dogs, a recent addition to the family, is batshit, as we say, and to any little creature—squirrel, bunny, puppy, cat—she lunges and screams, I mean she *screams*, like she's being scalded or having her skin peeled from her or something, and though it seems to me the scream is murderous, I guess it's possible it is a scream of curiosity and collegiality. Either way, Daisy's not hanging around to find out.

Daisy's foundational inquiry, her primary and abiding question, is whether or not the coast is clear, which, because we live in a neighborhood of cats, it's often not. Zeke and Zora, brother and sister, are the neighbor cats. Zora talks like a rusty swing set, and a lot. Zeke had been for a few years—until Gizmo's arrival—the sole baddest dude on this block. Zeke walks slow, and luxuriously, almost princely. They both kick Daisy's ass. Turmeric is a recent addition to Zeke and Zora's house, whose human mother claimed her from a junkyard in Indy hoping against hope that she was Ginger, the former bad-ass matriarch of the neighborhood who one day disappeared. She's not. Not even close. Toothless now because of some kind of mouth disease, and it seems to me with a bum leg or two, she also kicks Daisy's ass.

Gizmo is the deaf Siamese cat who moved across the street a couple years back, who's a little bit like Omar from *The Wire*, the streets mostly clear when he pokes his head from his cat door, and by the time he's trotted down the steps it's a ghost town, except one time Zeke stayed put, thickening up his coat and getting low, looking just past Gizmo, and Gizmo, slightly smaller than Zeke but wiry, sauntered directly to Zeke, getting lower with each step and looking also just past him, and when they got within spitting distance they started howling, at which point, on my porch, I put my book all the way down on my lap, for I knew it was soon to be on. I guess I could've broken it up, but, I'm sorry to tell you, I like to watch MMA. I was curious. When they commenced to brawling, it was straight out of *Tom and Jerry*. In the first round, they whirled about four feet into the air clutching each other in a kind of corkscrew motion. After a fifteen-second intermission, they jumped back on each other, and this time it was somersaults a few feet into the air, after which Zeke back-pedaled slowly, probably saying stuff like, *You're lucky I didn't sleep good last night*, and *You're lucky I had a sore paw*, etc., before scampering away. Needless to say, Gizmo sometimes kicks Daisy's ass.

There's that chubby homebody cat, whose name I don't know, across the street beneath the pear tree who never leaves her yard but would surely kick Daisy's ass. Then there's Baby Jake, like Paris from *The Iliad*, gorgeous, regal, always in the cut, seems mostly to be in seductive repose, who, when he moves, flounces. If it doesn't interfere with his preening, he kicks Daisy's ass. And finally there's Crazy Jake, Baby Jake's dad—sometimes we see them catching up in the alley—a true wildcat with matted fur who crawls almost like a snake and sleeps under our garage in a dugout with a woodchuck. Crazy Jake, I'm pretty sure, is Daisy's friend, her counselor, her confidant, her Yoda. A few times I've seen them lying on the same wall, no hackles, working things through.

All to say, Daisy's often on edge. Though I've not had my ass beat daily like she has, I have for other reasons at times in my life been all brain stem, all anxiety, all darting eyes and every sound coming for your throat, and so how lucky it feels to have her snuggled down, relaxed, safe, on my lap, purring so hard I can feel it into my chest, and when I take a sip of coffee or turn the page of my book and so stop petting her for a second, she puts her hand on my wrist and looks into my eyes as though to say, *Please don't stop.* A plea I feel lucky to heed.

(Aug. 19)

10. *Alright Baby!*

MY FRIEND BERNARDO and I went to the courts yesterday, and as we were running through our warm-up (about a hundred mid-range jumpers), a couple young guys came over and asked us to play—challenged us, it felt like, sort of lingering nearby, glaring at us a little derisively, it seemed, for the very act of warming up, *look at these dorks*—and when we finished warming up—oh fine, limbering up—and checked the ball in, we promptly kicked the shit out of them. My bad: we got more buckets than they did. These kids were in their early twenties, babies, though the baby who was guarding me—a wiry little guard in a snuggly of tattoos with a nice crossover and awful jump shot and reluctance to smile—was doing his damnedest to prove he was no baby. He was shoving me and elbowing me and wrapping me up and hacking me, all of which I was admiring, to myself and out loud. But when I blew a chippy jump hook and got my own rebound and was putting it back, he shoved me hard square in the chest and, being airborne, I fell inelegantly on my ass, though kept my eyes on the shot, which, damn, I missed.

When I was still on the ground, Bernardo and I made the briefest eyes at each other that held the entire history of mankind, by which I mean *man*-kind, the beginning middle and end of every war ever made, but I almost immediately jumped up and applauded this kid for a good hard foul, and even sort of hugged him, just this side of consensually, which he warily accepted, barking as I was a slurry of coachly affirmations—*Good stuff! Well done! Alright baby! That's what I'm talking about!*—which, in retrospect, were probably directed at me as much as my assailant. By which I mean it was not too long ago that if this baby—or any baby—hacked me like that so openly and notoriously, I would have thrown at least one punch in the direction of this baby's head. More accurately it would have been my body, my youthfully-testicled body, my youthful testicles, doing the throwing, throwing themselves toward this kid's head, which, you know, things can escalate; testicled things, *testicles*, can really go wrong.

But not today, for not only did my testicles feel no urge to throw themselves at this kid—which, and this time it's true, would've hurt me more than it would've him—*I felt myself feel* nothing like rage or embarrassment or hurt or, god forbid, disrespect (the scrotum's bread and butter). Better yet, and it seems to me this ought to be the scrotums's bread and butter, I felt love for this little tough guy, and I *felt myself feeling* love for this little tough guy, so much love I'm pretty sure it was also for my own little tough guy, getting less tough, and littler, by the day.

(Aug. 20)

11. The Full Moon!

FRIENDS, I AM forty-seven years old, nearly a half century of living under my belt, and it was only today, reading about herbs and tinctures and planting schedules and various other astro-agronomical affairs, that I learned, I am so shy to admit it to you, that the moon wanes into blank. I knew it waxed into full, but the waning part into no moon, which they call *new* moon, somehow eluded me, which I'm guessing it didn't you. You probably learned it, and kept it learned, in fourth grade or something. Not me. For some reason I was under the impression, clearly not the observational impression, that it goes from super bright (full, werewolves and such) to off. Like hitting a light switch.

I mean, look: I am only now learning this despite the fact that, among other things that might have hipped me (like my eyes), despite the cognitive acrobatics I have been doing to keep my understanding in place (like not believing my eyes), I believe 1000 percent that the moon, given as it affects the waves in the ocean, and given as we are mostly ocean, affects us profoundly. The moon may have chosen a few of the words in that last sentence. I am all the way on that team, and have been for a little while now, even though I was quite slow getting there, committed atheistico-materialist I aspired to be, pretending (or hoping?) everything was a machine that could be parsed and tinkered and decoded and conquered and possessed by the human intellect, figured out, I guess, myself especially I wonder (no luck). What is that about?

I mean, my god, I wonder if I would've been in my youth a congregant in the Bill Gates et al church of the-earth-is-a-halfwit-machine-we-can-outsmart-i.e.-lube-up-to-make-spin-better. (And-make-a-killing-while-pretending-to-do-so.) I really wonder. Maybe kinda I was. Though wayward, or black-sheepishly, given as I could never not take my dreams seriously. Given as though I refused palm readers and astrologers and their occult ilk because, I testified, I didn't believe them, it's really because I believe them.

Anyhow, alas, thanks to my boundless, bottomless, boundaryless ignorance: goddamn and holy shit!

Waxing and waning! Have you heard?!?! The world again is made to me anew, which, in a certain kind of way, my friend Penelope explained to me, if I heard this right, is how Descartes thought about *wonder*: wonder requires the novel, or the new, he said. He also evidently said wonder is without a companion or opposite emotion, the way happiness has sadness, and excitement has lethargy, etc. In this and probably some other things I disagree with Descartes, because wonder's opposite emotion is know-it-all-ery. The know-it-all's job is to put a stake in wonder's fat and gooey heart. Nothing new under the sun, etc. Which, of course, most everything is—new—or becomes so when we look longer or closer. And so—in addition to touching toes, expressing need, speaking in tongues, getting everything all over the place—wonder, being perpetually wonderst(r)uck, is another thing the very young are our gurus at. It's why they walk so damn slow. And never stop with the questions.

(Aug. 26)

12. Shortcut

ON WHAT MIGHT be unhyperbolically, uncontroversially, incontrovertibly one of the luckiest days in all of human existence, I was getting ready to hop on my bike to get a coffee and work on some essays, but as I was rolling my bike from the house, I remembered that my rear tire had gone flat of its own accord the night before, leaning against the bookshelf, suddenly exhaling down to the rim. So I reversed my bike back to its place, and took off on foot. I moseyed through the neighborhood, past Jeff and Amy's, past Sully's, past Sarah's, past a house whose kousa dogwood was dropping its prickly, sweet fruit, two of which I picked up from the ground and ate. I crossed Second Street—oh, I'm talking to my mother on the phone; today I'm *that* guy—past a ruin that would, with a broom, be in no time a great skate spot; past the trailer park; over to First, where yesterday, as I was walking by, my friend Kayte gave me a huge and yummy carrot that she pulled from fluffy soil before my eyes—voila!; and past her neighbor's, my friend Michael's, yard, where he was shoveling some mulch.

Michael has a big fig tree I much envy; I have fig envy, I'm not afraid to admit it, mine never get all the way big, nor do they get all the way ripe, like Michael's do. Michael's figs get big and ripe on the southwest corner of his house, baking there as they like, and so I asked my mom to hold on a sec—probably she feels like she's been holding on a sec for her kids for her whole life; there she is jangling her keys again—while I admired the tree to Michael, who then rooted around in the big leaves that looked like hands cheering or hands waiting to catch something and found for me a ripe, purple fig, handing it to me while making a face like the transmission of great wisdom was afoot, or like he was handing me a key, which I tucked in my pocket for later. When I pointed to the phone and mouthed *My mom*, Michael smiled and said, quietly, *Oh, hi Mom!*

I carried on down Dodds, to the coffee shop whose patio was too full for working, it was a zone of interruption, which is somedays what I want. But today I wanted a zone of public solitude (a paradox perhaps you can relate to?), a zone to tune up some sentences. So I continued on Dodds, and it felt like divine providence that just past Washington on the left I saw, *holy shit holy shit*, another beautiful stand of figs, this one even more abundant than Michael's, because it's actually about five or six stands of figs, all of them with nearly ripe and swollen fruit. I was envying and observing the tree when Alan, half of the couple who parent these trees, and whom I know only cursorily, came out and immediately asked if I wanted any. Really, it was like, *Oh, hi Ross, want some figs? Hell yeah*, I said, and as we shuffled the leaves to find three big ripe ones, Ann, the other parent, joined us. As we were talking, she let slip that she had only recently had her first pawpaw despite being from Indiana, where the fruit grows plentifully in the woods and is aptly named, because it tastes something like a banana, the Indiana banana.

I thanked them for the figs, continued up Dodds to Hillside, toward the other café, the alone together rather than together together café, passing along the way a magnolia tree that droops over the sidewalk, making a complete canopy, little bars of light dropping through as the branches reach like they're ready to scoop you up, to embrace you. *Thank you*, I said to the magnolia, ducking on my way out, for it was about ten degrees cooler under there, and it's a hot one.

After I wrote sentences and drank coffee, I texted my friend Alex to see if I could grab some pawpaws, which his place has in abundance. I mean, ABUNDANCE. *C'mon*, he texted back. I passed on my way a pear tree leaning over the sidewalk, from which I grabbed two, knocked on the door, and handed Alex the bigger of the pears, and two of my four figs. He was glad for the pear, and freaked for the figs. Then we walked around the house to the stately, pyramidal, dense, tall trees, loaded beyond my dreams. I mean, when I walked into the dark canopy of the pawpaws to grab some fallen fruit—for this is how you harvest pawpaws, they are like persimmons this way: you pick them up from the ground—I immediately stepped on one. It only halfway smooshed, so I grabbed and gobbled it, caramelly sweet. I picked up a few other sweet little monsters, and Alex brought from inside the house a tub halfway full of pawpaws he'd already harvested, overwhelmed with the bounty of these trees. (Pro tip for you renters out there; if you can, rent a place with a healthy and prolific fruit tree, or three.) I grabbed ten or so from his tub, which, in addition to the five I'd already picked up, made fifteen hearty, ripe pieces of fruit, which I gently placed in my backpack, distributing them so they might not moosh in there. The whole while we chatted, we worried, we despaired that it had just rained in Northern Greenland.

I told him my rage was florid. *Your rage is what?* he asked. *Florid*, I said. *My rage feels florid.* Alex's seven-year-old child ran by as I heaved my backpack of fruit onto my shoulders.

I thanked Alex and walked the back way through an alley the half block or so to Ann and Alan's, the fig parents, to drop off five pawpaws, for which they offered me some cookies, but I lied and said I was in a sugar-free stint, because I worry sometimes vegan sounds like a judgment, and I hate vegan judgment. Then down Grant, a left down Second, right on Walnut, to where the new parking garage is, not all the way open, with big plastic barriers to prevent pedestrians from cutting through which, being reasonable, they shoved out of the way, for who in their right mind doesn't sometimes love a shortcut?

(Sept. 12)

13. Babies Again (Seriously)

WHO CARES REALLY what you think of babies, whether you find them a blessing, a bore, a bramble, a key, a window, a door, a wormhole, a wonder, a Whac-a-Mole, a babble, a blather, adorbs, or a bad idea (hint: all of the above)? It doesn't matter. Because, you will agree, today our sole job is noticing, and if you're me, *admiring,* this squirt riding her mother's hip, not only because she immediately threw her hand up at me to wave, smiling in that puzzled baby way, somewhat flummoxed I suspect by the action she has suddenly occasioned in this bizarre flesh ball she's inhabiting and whose compliance she is only just realizing she can sometimes achieve, but also because when she passed me, and I was then on the other side of her mother, who is these days, among other things probably (handmaid, surgeon, sippy cup, meal, medicine, militia, napkin, professor, pillow, bidet, bouncehouse, chaise lounge, champion), her chariot, she turned her little head to the rear, behind her, to keep eye contact with me, to keep waving, and I was of course so stoked and enamored and impressed with the little bald animal throwing her tiny hand at me that I likewise compelled my body to wave, again and again. And the child, polite, befuddled, humoring me by now, also did it again, same face—curiosity, alacrity, sweetness, stoked—and same hand, she was a righty.

(Sept. 16)

14. *Animalympics*

AS I WAS walking home today, a young woman ran by me, making a left on Fourth, and I swear to you she had the exact running form as René Fromage—high elbows tight to the body, heel-toe stride close to the ground, slightly jutting chin—the French marathoner goat from *Animalympics*, the feature-length cartoon from 1980. This kid was probably about twenty, so would not have been born, or even a glimmer in mom's tummy, when Fromage was competing, nor his nemesis, Kit Mambo, the lioness from . . . well, she may have been from the country of Africa. That's how it was in the eighties, you remember the pre-post-colonial hit by Toto, don't you?

When I think of early eighties pop-cultural racial/national/sexual, etc., indoctrinations, *Animalympics* was pretty gentle in its deployments, as opposed to the WWF, with which I and every boy I knew was obsessed, and every Saturday morning we'd study the Wild Samoans, Kamala the Ugandan Giant (did they really say he was a cannibal?), the Iron Sheik (from Iran, his move was the Camel Clutch), his commie Russian tag-teammate Nikolai Volkoff (who sang the Russian national anthem, to maniacal boos), Mr. Fuji (who threw salt in people's eyes), Rowdy Roddy Piper (Scottish-ish racist dude), the Missing Link (from parts unknown, i.e., he was biracial), and Junkyard Dog, a black dude who came to the ring wearing a dog collar with a chain around his neck—at least he usually held on to the chain as I recall, which is a step up I guess?—and he barked as much as he spoke.

My brother and I probably watched *Animalympics* on the newly invented HBO about ten million times. It vies for emotional heft in my imagination only with *Dot and the Kangaroo*, about a little girl who goes missing in Australia's outback and is saved by a mom kangaroo whose joey has gone missing. I won't spoil the ending, but I'll tell you this: I cried. A lot. But as for *Animalympics*, I'm telling you, I could sing all the songs, especially the melancholy ones—I'm just built like that—including the tune (a kind of early music video, in fact) by which we learn René Fromage's backstory, his conversion from Parisian Existentialist Café Loafer to dedicated, monomaniacal Olympic marathoner who forsakes all the enticements of the world—goat women, croissants, money—for his one and only goal, the gold medal, which, get ready for it now, by the end of the music video, spoiler alert, turns into Kit Mambo!

More spoiler alert, and here's why *Animalympics* is the best feature-length cartoon movie of all time, after, of course, the *Peanuts* movies (*A Boy Named Charlie Brown* and *Race for Your Life Charlie Brown!* especially): René Fromage would not win the gold by himself. Nor would his ostensible adversary, Kit Mambo (who, incidentally, I was rooting for, needless to say). Because they fell in love and ran the last part of the race holding hands, their significantly different gaits synched perfectly up, and they crossed the finish line at the exact same time, *they shared the gold*, which not only caused their coaches to go batshit, it was also a preemptive alternative, an otherwise to the coked-up, cutthroat, capitalistic, crabs-in-a-barrel shitfest end-times you might have noticed blooming just outside your window. Or, less luckily, inside it.

(Sept. 22)

15. Under the Table

TODAY I WAS talking to someone about a job they were thinking of taking, and it paid fine, not great but it was under the table, which is a little better. Under the table, as you know, means to be paid unreportedly, sub rosa, untaxed, and oh, this one I forgot—*off the books*. Strange to rarely use this phrase anymore, given how frequently we said it in my youth, almost constantly from the time the kids in our neighborhood were of working age until about fifteen years ago, at which point I became salaried (aside from a yearlong stint hustling kettlecorn). Prior to this, like most people everywhere forever, I usually worked for cash, or cash-adjacent (checks or goodies). Whether bussing tables at the Country Club one New Year's, or shoveling snow around the apartments, or raking leaves down in Hulmeville, or parking cars at the racetrack, or delivering papers or painting houses or hanging drywall or cleaning out the house of someone's deceased mother, or moving (and sometimes breaking) art, or, more recently and for a little spell, working construction with my buddy, who maybe felt some kind of way about commerce in our friendship, something a little filthy perhaps, because, as I recall, he never placed the money directly in my hand, but instead always tossed it, already counted out, usually unfolded, on a surface between us—car seat, kitchen table—while expressing, heartily, his appreciation.

Before that, my first sustained experience of under-the-table employment, aside from the paper route, which I did from age ten to about twenty (though that seems a different kind of off the books, off the comic books, maybe), was when I worked at a pizzeria shortly after my sophomore year of football and basketball—I mean *high school*—for which I was endeavoring to gain weight, which they aided and abetted by passing my way every single burnt pizza or messed up or unclaimed cheesesteak or hoagie or meatball sub, etc. And when Paolo, the owner, called dinnertime, if I got sucked into scrubbing the grimy pipes beneath the sink or making the sauce in that huge vat—stirring it with my bare arm like I was shown by someone with hairier arms than I would ever have, this was the old country now—and as a consequence was a little bit slow reporting to the booth where we ate the family-style dishes Paolo prepared that were not on the menu, he would scream and sometimes pound the table for me to get out there to eat with them right now, which I did.

Six bucks an hour under the table, ooh, that was nice. I made $3.75 an hour at Burger King down the street about a year earlier, where the manager threatened once to throw me through the drive-thru window, which, maybe not for me but for the adults with families who made the same, is called being bent over the table, which might be an inappropriate way of saying a true thing. They were also so kind in the Kingdom, in addition to the twenty-five bucks for eight hours of work before taxes, as to give you half off your meal, which is why we stole everything we could. If you came through the drive-thru as a friend, you might get a bacon-quintuple cheeseburger or a sixty-piece chicken tenders. It was, although inversely so, a similar logic by which, if you were an asshole when you ordered, you might've gotten some snot or spit in your burger, which, among fifteen-year-old boys, is the very most benign of possible bodily condiments.

I am always looking for a place to laud who steals (back) from their shitty employer—I think my nana told us about some shoes she got off the woman she was a domestic for, who probably didn't pay her great. My dad would often bring home fish and French fries when he was working at Red Lobster. My buddy Walt used to steal filet mignon from the country club where he worked, which we would then grill and debase on white buns with ketchup with ironic, blasphemal glee. And Poppa, who was dying the last twenty years of his life (Wait, aren't we all? No no, not like that; dude was always just about to die, he had everything, he was, turns out, unkillable, until he died), when he fell from a stool in his son's kitchen and broke his hip asked his son, *Son, would it be okay with you if I sue you?* to which my uncle, his son, suggested he ought not, though Poppa made a good case: *It's not gonna hurt you, Son, it's just the insurance company.* Granted, the insurance company was not to my Poppa exactly a shitty employer, but close enough that I still applaud the ingenuity, the indecent proposal. The rich write the laws so they don't have to break them to steal from the rest of us.

And yet it never in a million years would have occurred to me to have stolen from Paolo, because we had, what's it called, oh yeah, a *relationship*. He asked me how football was going (I mean school); he showed me how to cook cheesesteaks and meatball parms, how to toast the bun right and to melt the cheese so it doesn't burn; he only let Italians do pizza, but he let me do the dough and the sauce; he called my mother Momma and sometimes wouldn't take her money; he fed me well and *never* took my money for doing so and he sent me home weekly with a wad of cash I would not have to share with the current suite of American wars (even if I was more concerned at the time with my kicks and my Drakkar Noir). Way more money than the assholes down the street at the Kingdom would ever pay me, which, and oh how it delights me to tell you, that wretched outpost anyway, that particular weepy sore, is no more.

(Oct. 1)

16. Hole in the Head, Redux; Coda: Negreeting

IF *THE BOOK OF DELIGHTS* is at all interesting, it is only as interesting as it is cognizant of, and sometimes straining against, the enticing and ample *Book of* Un*delights*, which I was reminded of when a woman on a Zoom reading asked me to talk a little bit about the fourth essay in *The Book of Delights*, called "Hole in the Head," in which I recount having learned, from the emailed trailer of a documentary (*email*: oft the vector of undelight) about a radiation experiment on little black children that took place an hour and change from where I live, in Southern Indiana. The subject of that documentary, Vertus Hardiman, had a baseball-sized hole burned into his head from the procedure. How polite of me to put into passive voice what those people, those doctors and nurses, at the behest surely of some corporation or other, some shareholders, some authority, did to little Vertus: they burned a hole in his head. On account of which unrare brutality I write, *Dear Lord, black people, please do not let a white person in a lab coat experiment on you or your children. Dear Lord.*

In what was a kind of negreeting,[1] this woman explained she was asking because many of the schools in our country are preparing to mandate an experimental drug for kids the age of her own children, about which she had what I would consider some very reasonable parental, and nonpartisan, apprehension. Apprehension that, whether you share it or not, seems to me anyway, could only be incomprehensible to you, could only be *Oh my god what are they thinking, oh my god trust the science*, via a studied and committed refusal to acknowledge, or commitment to forget, this little thing called the history of science, which overlaps with the history of medicine, wherein, in addition to plenty of really good stuff, plenty of bad stuff, like *really* bad stuff, has been done, and *is always being done*, to us.

---

1 A greeting, often subtle, between two black people. See: Gay, *The Book of Delights,* p. 23.

Some of us more than others, yes, but most of us, one way or another.

One of the results of which is a kind of understanding, a wisdom, which I sometimes think of as epigenetic suspicion (which overlaps, incidentally, with epigenetic *care*), or not always trusting those who call themselves the authorities. The absence of which suspicion, or the profusion of such unwavering trust—I'm not talking about what we decide to do, whether by choice or, often, coercion; I'm talking about *what we think* and *how we feel*—especially among those to whom really bad stuff has been or is being done again and again and again, which, to reiterate, is most of us, seems to me, as I suspect it did to my interlocutor, fucking bonkers.

By which I think I mean confusing. And by confusing, I mean frightening. And in addition to frightening, I mean sad, like truly heartbreaking, how quickly we can be convinced to loathe and exile and fire and throw out of school and such each other, and sometimes I think the loathing is provoked, or stoked, to distract us from acknowledging, which might then mean understanding, which might then mean addressing, or confronting, the numerous *causes* for suspicion and distrust of the authorities, which might include, in addition to all those aforementioned holes in heads (*very* abbreviated list here; like, *very*): being the descendant of people who were treated as property; having been driven from your land; having had your neighborhood razed for a highway or an industrial park; having had the top of the mountain where you live blown off; having been disbelieved, or brutalized, in a medical setting; being lied into wars; being lied to by politicians as a matter of course; how they're kinda always lying; how so many elected officials, public servants they're called, are really rich, and how they hang out with really rich people, whose interests they seem to share; having had the jobs shipped away and the unions broken up; that all the dumps and oil refineries and derailments are in the poor neighborhoods; how much easier it is to buy a soda or chips than spinach or beans; how an ad for a hypertension or cholesterol drug might follow one for fast food; that they're kinda always lying; the imprisonment industry; how expensive they make it to be broke; who all they've murdered and put in jail; the apparently booming dialysis and plasma donation (i.e., blood-selling) industries; that the federal minimum wage is still $7.25; the ongoing and intentional opioid disaster; how our healthcare system seems far more interested in illness than in prevention, let alone *health*; how as the number of billionaires increase so, too, do the number of homeless (probably suicides and overdoses and mass shootings etc., too); how in some towns (probably not

Scarsdale or Beverly Hills or Montclair) the water will give you brain damage, and it might even catch fire; that they're kinda always lying; that ours is and always has been a system (but if you're a teacher, don't you dare put this in your curriculum in a growing number of states!) that depends upon having, and making us complicit in having, and making us content with and by having, an expendable population to whom anything, by which we both know I mean *anything*, can be done.

And the more we're tricked into loathing one another, the more it will be.

(Oct. 6)

17. The Lady in the Tree

I HAD JUST put in my laundry at the laundromat and as I was sitting on the curb in the sun, looking across the parking lot, I heard but did not see a woman yell, "A girl, right?" And a brown dude, walking beneath the voice and pushing a baby stroller, turned the chariot to the woman, who was, now I could tell, obscured by a tree, and so her voice—a white Hoosier voice with a touch of the East, a little pinch of Jersey or Philly back there, which, gotta say, smooths out my hackles some—seemed to be coming from the tree. This brown dude, who, pretty sure, was not a black dude—which I think I gathered, stay with me, from his footwear: a certain kind of sandal; very thin, possibly leather, with a loop over the toe—was darker-skinned than me, although I am, in common parlance (in many parts of this country, anyway, though the world overall is an entirely different ballgame), a black dude. Race is like God; it'll do whatever you need it to.

Dude turned his baby girl to the white woman shouting to him from up in the tree, something about Halloween, which, what do I know?, a thousand assumptions a second, this dude ain't trick or treating, and she said "*something something* beautiful, *something something* precious," and he seemed not to be saying anything, though I could see him looking up into the tree, nodding. A somewhat reticent or guarded smile. And I heard from the tree something like "hair ties," and then the brown dude nodded, his baby girl still tilted on her rear wheels, and then it was quiet for a second and the brown dude rested the carriage back down on all four wheels before taking a few steps to his right, where he bent over to pick up whatever the woman threw down from the tree, I'm guessing some hair ties for his beautiful, precious baby girl. After he grabbed the hair ties, he waved to the tree with the same hand that was holding the gift, and the woman in the tree said something like "Okay baby" as the man turned his carriage and baby girl to carry on their way, immediately after which she hollered at this big, burly white dude in a camo hat leaning against a phone pole across the street, "You okay?," which he didn't quite look. But he smiled, too, I could see it beneath his camo cap, and he nodded, and gave the tree a thumbs up.

(Oct. 8)

18. The Lady on the Porch

THIS IS ONE of those days the book isn't big enough, because in the intervening forty-five minutes the white-voiced lady in the tree has spoken to literally every single person who has gone by—every single one—which is up to about thirteen, if I was counting right. My nana always loved to sit on her porch, regardless of where she lived, probably because she loved being a black-voiced lady in the tree, dispensing goodies and advice and compliments and critiques and hair ties and such. My nana loved talking shit at the world.

Nana also like to sit on the porch, she said, probably because her last name was Porch, from her third husband, who, my mother reports, wasn't great, though I never met him. I knew her first husband, my father's father, who I knew as Poppa. And her second husband I met once, at their son's funeral. Keith died of a heart attack at thirty-five. When I was having some heart stuff and they did a family history I was like, *Nope, nope*, and then I called my brother to double-check and we remembered Uncle Keith, and when I said, *You know, I had an uncle . . . should I put that down?*, they said, *Yeah, you probably should*. Nana's second husband, Mr. Turner, like Keith, was tall, dark brown, very handsome, with pretty hands. But about Nana's third husband, Porch, the one I never met, my mom's beef, like my nana's incidentally, was that he was always playing golf instead of working. I have no beef with not working, though I do have beef with golf.

It sounds like Nana is maybe, at last, truly on her way—she's ninety-six, and all three of her siblings, aged ninety-nine to ninety, are alive—in a nursing home in Youngstown, no longer able to get out of bed, very tired, you can let go, Nana, it's been a long time. About a decade ago, when I was visiting her in her high-rise old folks' home across from the Cleveland Clinic, in addition to flirting hard with some man in the elevator (*You got a car? Because I don't mess with no man without a car.*) and boasting about how a couple nights prior she had been at a geriatric dance-off and was by far the best one down there, she bragged me up and down the hallways, telling the other old folks *This is my baby*, and *He's a writer*, and telling everyone she made me greens without the ham hock *because he doesn't eat meat and still they're good*. We went to Corky & Lenny's out on Chagrin Boulevard just past Shaker Heights, where Nana got a pastrami and I got a veggie burger (which they for some reason kindly made a double) and she told me the waitress was flirting with me. She dipped her French fry into the ketchup and pointed it at my double, then giggled, the wispy way she did, *She's trying to get with you, Rossy*. Takes one to know one I guess.

We came back to sit on her sixth-floor porch overlooking the parking lot, where she was growing peppers and tomatoes and greens in pots. She was telling me about her momma's garden—just like I am incapable of calling my father's mother anything but Nana, my nana was incapable, it seemed, of calling her mother anything but Momma—before she excused herself for a second and came back with a bag of goodies from what she called, pretty sure, the hunger center. Inside was a cheap electric toothbrush (she grabbed two), some store-brand toothpaste (she grabbed two), some beans, and some spaghetti. *Baby, could you use this?* she asked, and though I didn't really need it, I said *yes please* and *thank you*.

Oh, but I also wanted to mention that after listening to the lady in the tree for a while, I went back in to change my laundry and noticed the third of my three machines was empty—I figured the attendant maybe moved my clothes somewhere, but when I asked, she told me she didn't know, then went into detective mode. She eventually figured, opening a washer a few doors down and seeing some granny panties in there, *A ha! That lady must've taken your clothes.* We laughed together, considering that granny finding my clothes, which, though I'm shedding some pounds through these times, they ain't gonna kill me like that, I'm still six four, and my clothes on that lady will be very big. My clothes will make that granny a baby.

Lord, I believe in almost nothing anymore, except these fleeting sweetnesses, these dime-a-dozen precious sweetnesses, these sweetnesses that seem to me the organizing fact of our lives, or maybe more accurately the reasons to stay alive, these people in trees and on porches and in laundromats taking my phone number for when my clothes came back. And while I was giving her my number, a woman standing guard next to her washer (good idea!) reading her phone, who I'd noticed glancing up periodically at our conversation, called out, looking down still at her phone, but smiling, *That's life in the laundromat!*

(Oct. 8)

19. How Good It Feels

I WAS WALKING to retrieve my bike from my office, where I left it last night because it was pouring, and on my route I passed, as I often do, for I am a creature of habit and my grooves run deep, a porch where a young man is often stationed, and I can often tell whether or not he is stationed there by the smell of cigarette smoke ambling up the road. Though he sometimes waves, it's barely, and he doesn't seem well. Which maybe I recognize in part because though at this moment I feel well enough—in fact I feel well—I have had years of feeling very unwell, densely so.

I remember laughing with my friend Wendy at the notion that anyone might not have had the desire, even if only flickeringly, to jump out the window or in front of the tractor trailer. That anyone might not understand—I didn't say *approve of*, I said *understand*; and understanding, at least for me (and I bet Wendy) makes the idea of approval in this context childish—how someone needed to throw themselves off something. I guess it's a kind of relief, by which I mean both an emotional state and a raised image made by carving away the negative space, that this poem of Gabrielle Calvocoressi's gets at: "[. . .] I did not / want to die that day. Oh, my God. / Why don't we talk about it? How good it feels. / And if you don't know then you're lucky / but also you poor thing. Bring the band out on the stoop. / Let the whole neighborhood hear. [. . .]"

All of which is to say, today dude was playing on a boom box (delight: the onomatopoetic word and fact: *boom box*)—so loud the whole block could hear, and dance to if we wanted—Prince's "1999."

Can we talk about it?

(Oct. 11)

20. Braces on Adults

A COUPLE UNDERGRADS were walking in my direction on campus today, chatting and smiling, and at some point, they started laughing hard, kind of leaning into one another, and as they got close to me, then passed, I noticed that one of them had braces on his teeth, which, in anyone not a child, makes me a puddle. There is something so dear about this adult endeavor toward—what, a better smile, less dental pain, greater jaw health, enunciatory support?—that, for whatever reason—lack of access, lack of diagnosis, lack of time, lack of concern—is not endeavored toward until adulthood. I have a friend my age who is always fiddling around with the rubber bands in his mouth, he has some sort of midlife orthodontics happening, and if he eats, he takes them out, without saying so, the way some people surreptitiously down a few pills at meals without saying so. The way I used to hit my inhaler once or twice a day even on good days, until I got off dairy. When the frailty of the adult human animal becomes for whatever reason evident, perhaps especially the adult human *male* animal, whose frailty is for that creature often a source of shame, it can almost make me cry. I guess the braces is that on steroids, because piled atop the frailty (crooked teeth) is this other thing boys sometimes (shamefully) want, too, which is to be cute.

My buddy Don, before he was murdered, told me he was excited about having at last a steady and secure job with insurance, perhaps for the rest of his life—quick one: for whomever thinks of tenure as an obscene privilege, I would like to blow your mind with this alternative perspective: What if we all had tenure and three months off and parental leave and a library and comfortable-ish chairs at the job site?—in part because he wanted to get his teeth fixed because, like so many people, he probably spent years uninsured, and definitely dentally uninsured. He smiled when he said it, pulling his bottom lip down to show me his crooked teeth. It was very cute.

Unlike this kid on campus, unlike my buddy fiddling with his rubber bands at lunch, unlike dear Don in some parallel life I sometimes imagine for him, alive and down the block and coming over unannounced for dinner and with braces on those lower teeth, I never had braces, never needed them, for my teeth came out, or came in, I guess, pretty straight, though my mother chipped in, too. By which I mean the time I was swinging too high—I was always swinging too high—on the shopping cart corral at Sears Surplus down off Roosevelt Boulevard while my mother was inside shopping, which was the bane of my existence, and because I became the bane of hers when I was dragged along, she'd be more than happy if we would play out in the parking lot, good and sane parenting for which she might now be arrested, or put on a list. She also left us in the car when we were little sometimes, to grab some milk and, it's like a miracle or something, we survived.[1] Anyway,

---

1 I would be remiss, though, to omit that one time my mother parked the car right in front of the convenience store, close enough she could see us the whole time as she ran in to get some milk—isn't it always milk they're running in to get, maybe eggs?—leaving my big brother and me inside (sans car seats *or* seat belts!), which I guess upset me (either her being gone, or our still being in her sight, not sure), so I started crying. My brother tried with his voice and probably hands to soothe me, it wouldn't be the last time, telling me it'd be okay and such, he's good like that, was always looking out for me. But when the more conventional modes of soothing didn't work, he tried the cigarette lighter, placing it on my pointer finger, which didn't exactly soothe me, though it took my mind from whatever had been bugging me. That, too, we survived, as did our relationship. Though I keep my distance from him when he has ignitory tools in hand, I feel as close to him as ever. Which, you won't be surprised, makes our mom, whom I call Ol' Ma, so, so glad.

as I was having a good time swinging, my feet went a tad too high, my arms couldn't hold, and I fell face first onto the cement sidewalk below.

Matty, my brother, swinging, too, albeit less rambunctiously—my brother was always the albeit less rambunctious one—walked me into the store, blood pouring from my face, which I barely noticed because I couldn't see through all the stars. My mother barked at Matty to *get him out of here he's gonna bleed on the clothes* (we weren't flush like that; it's why we were at the Surplus), which he did, guiding me by my elbow back to near the scene of the crime, where our mother met us, as usual a little bit pissed off. She really never got a minute. But she quickly saw my face was caved in and she softened, taking my hand and walking me over to the Dunkin Donuts across the parking lot, where she escorted me and my bloody, caved-in face through the store to the women's bathroom in the back, and got to work.

But in order to get in there, because my lower teeth had gone through my lower lip and were stuck like that, she had to remove my teeth, which luckily were still intact, from my lip, or my lip from my teeth, or something gross whatever it was. Once she got that out of the way, she looked into my mouth, made a quick call (my mother grew up on a farm, and it's to that tutelage

I attribute this facility; she won states in Minnesota for killing, dressing, and preparing a chicken in 1958) reached into my mouth, felt that my lower teeth had all been shoved back quite a ways, and proceeded, with her first two fingers, to drag those teeth, which sounded to me like an earth mover changing a landscape, back into place. She pulled my bloody, punctured lip down to check her work, which smarted, tugged a little here, shoved a little there, squinted the one eye, wet a paper towel in the sink, wiped my face, and said, *C'mon, let's go*. And she grabbed a dozen munchkins on the way out.

(Oct. 15)

21. (Foot- End- Etc.) Notes

KATHERINE MCKITTRICK'S BOOK *Dear Science and Other Stories* came in the mail today, along with Rebecca Solnit's *Recollections of My Nonexistence* and Geoff Dyer's *See/Saw*. I immediately started flipping through the McKittrick because I had heard from someone I work with that it was a weird book, I saw a weird talk of hers on YouTube confirming that it might be a weird book, and I love few things as much as I love a weird book. Also, my impression was that it was going to be a book by an academic that does not adhere to standards of academic writing, among which sometimes seems to be a commitment to profound, unbearable, and untenable boringness, which I think is the (often unwitting) result of the (often untroubled) belief in (and aspiration to) objectivity, a colonial, or at least *dominator*, and really childish crock of shit if there ever was one.

I once was among a group of fellows in residence for a year at the Radcliffe Institute for Advanced Study, a place that is part of Harvard, and though some people were impressed by the libraries and stuff, and whose pictures were on the walls, and names, I knew we were on a different planet when they told us we didn't have to put stamps on our outgoing mail when we sent it through the institute—the language was, more or less, *they have people for that.* A nonprofit planet with the endowment of a country, where most everything was free for us but the people in town have to pay to use the gym and the library. But that's not this story (though that is *the* story). While there, the writer Michael Pollan gave a little talk about writing for the fellows, many of whom were professors, wrote books, and adjudicated the writing of other impressionable people. When Pollan suggested that writing from a question instead of a thesis makes for more compelling writing and thinking, for reader and writer alike, eyeballs fell from heads. Elbow patches from corduroy jackets. Because the thesis (and the proof) are how writing is taught, which means it is how thinking is taught, and that leads to really bad, or boring at least, thinking. Another thing we go to school to learn. Whoops! Sidetracked!

To my delight I found that McKittrick's book is thoroughly footnoted, not only in a standard bibliographical way, though some of that, but in a digressive, contrapuntal, sub-argumentative way. By which I mean, quick glance here, it appears as though some of these footnotes are miniature essays, essayettes, which I'm sure complicate, deepen, twist up, who knows, the text. Occasionally these footnotes are a whole page or more. It might be the poet in me, by which I mean the writer obsessed with form in me, who is so interested in and enamored of the oddball overlong footnote, the footnote that calls into question the very idea of the ancillary, just as Jenny Boully's book *The Body*, made entirely of footnotes, does. I'm pretty sure the first time I realized I loved footnotes was Junot Dìaz's book *The Brief Wondrous Life of Oscar Wao*, where the author pokes his head through the curtains of the novel to give crucial lessons on the history of the Dominican Republic, etc. I was finishing a PhD, which some people call a PhDuh, and was relieved—thrilled really—to see someone making playful use of what is usually a toneless, utilitarian, citational requirement of the form (bad writing). I have lately been writing long footnotes myself—way too long, believe me—in an effort, I realized as they were accruing, to do that thing we do in conversation, which is interrupt ourselves, or interject—*oh yeah hold up you need to know this, too*—such that, in the best conversations, the ones I love, *visiting* is the word, you sometimes go as deep as you do far. Another poetic preoccupation, perhaps. Another definition of the lyric, perhaps. That's my two cents anyway.[1]

Cousin to my love for full-bodied, full-throated footnotes is my love of endnotes, the ones that serve the standard citational purpose, but I'm always looking, again, for the endnotes that refuse to end, which makes citation a kind of song, all these notes that want to keep the song going. Endnotes like how Luther Vandross ends (or doesn't) his version of "Superstar" or "A House Is Not a Home." How Erykah Badu's "Green Eyes" ends about four times, or maybe five. I imagine it's already happened, but given my own inclination to sometimes spend more time on the endnotes than on the body of the text—which maybe we should call the midnote?—I long for a book made of only endnotes. Which, if I was reading it, truth be told, after a page or two I'd go looking for some other notes, maybe the acknowledgments, which I just might love the most, and I have to admit it is often where I turn first when reading a book,

---

1 For another example of compelling footnotes, check out Samuel Delaney's book *Of Solids and Surds*, where he includes often quite funny, and always insightful, dialogue between his editor and himself about the proposed edits to the book.

which, it's true, when I was a young whippersnapper in the writing world, especially the petite and profoundly entangled poetry world, was because I probably wanted to know who the writer knew, by which I was likely doing some kind of petty recon: Was the pub the result of connections? Did the teacher get them the hookup? Etc. (Hint: yes. Even when no, yes.)[2]

But these days, freed for the time being from that particular need to position myself—to know who knows who knows who knows who knows; i.e., and strange, people might now sweat who knows me—I find myself reading the acknowledgments as a way to know *how* they know who they know (ooh, delight: *how* and *who* are anagrammatical pals). Some writers seem to fancy themselves solo travelers, some have a tight-knit crew they feel indebted to (close readers, family, friends, this or that fellowship or granting institution), and some go on and on and on and on.

2 When I receive my copy of the *Poetry Project Newsletter*, as good a literary publication as I know (and free!), I find myself spending most of my time on the feature called "Remembrances," where, you probably guessed it, people write about the recently deceased. It is so interesting to me, and moving, to listen to people talk about their recently departed. Probably a little extra interesting, too, since some of these now dead people's poems I have read, a lot of the poets I love have died (or are dying), and I, too, will one day be a dead poet. Anyhow, I mention it because this is another example of me flipping to the endnotes.

Little (literary) theory here: some of these ad nauseum acknowledgers, among whom I count myself, have spent a lot of time reading liner notes to records, but particularly hip-hop records, or cassettes and CDs in my case, which were exorbitant and vernacular in their gratitude. They were like maps of entanglement, or webs, some of which was legible to a visitor—Posdnuos thanking, for instance, Q-Tip or Monie Love or whoever—some of which was not, for I don't know his cousin's nickname, or the name of the dude who lent him the recording studio that weekend, or some other nearly secret thing. (The poet Willie Perdomo, by the way, is the John Coltrane of acknowledgments. "Acknowledgement" as mycelial love note.) But someone does. That's to say, acknowledgments, like the best writing, might not be perfectly *relatable*, as the kids say. Or better yet, *decipherable*. They might be a little bit like reading Greek, unless you're Greek, that is, or you have a Greek granny or lover, or maybe if you're Puerto Rican but you grew up in Astoria, or you grew up in Levittown but love *Clash of the Titans*, by which I really mean unless you understand being grateful for what has made *your song* possible, which I recommend we go on and on (and on and on) trying to be.

(Oct. 16)

22. Dream Dancing

IT IS TRUE, my dream life is a source of much contemplation, private and with whomever will listen, maybe even you, though I'll try not to overshare. Among last night's escapades: some almost romance (i.e., romantus interruptus); giving a talk for an audience who was way less enthused than I anticipated; and shaking someone's hand who said, while our hands were clasped, aghast, about hand shaking I think, *Oh I don't do that*. The last one seems like a COVID-era consent dream.

Though the dream of note for our purposes happened later, in another part of the dream—are dreams made of parts? segments? fragments? bones? viscera? particles? And what is the word for the undiscernible transitions or intermissions between those parts?—where I was on my way someplace else, probably a flight

I needed to catch, but got for some reason waylaid in a park where I started working on some dance moves that were, if I say so myself, kinda nice. The one move I remember working on was, in the day, called Around the World, and it's kind of like moonwalking in a circle, though I was also moving my arms and shoulders in a gangly cabbage patch. And when I was dancing, I spotted a couple kids on the other side of the park, maybe fifty or so yards away, also dancing, and working on similar moves. And when I saw these kids dancing, I thought to myself, in the dream, *Ha, I guess that's going to be my delight today, dancing by myself at the park and realizing I'm not actually dancing by myself at the park.* Though my dreams often—perhaps too often—infect my delights, this is the first instance of the delights infecting my dreams.

I don't recall us acknowledging each other, but we all knew the others were there, you know how that goes, dancing a little crisper because someone might be watching. You want to hear them think *Damn.* And as I was sliding over the cement, trying to make my feet glide more than slide, I spun and saw another crew of young folks, late teens to early twenties, dancing, in the same ballpark of moves, too. Same thing, acknowledgment communicated by dancing just a little bit crisper, the moves a little bit sharper. I was aware, self-conscious, of being an older fella dancing with these youngsters, but I carried on, and I think I was keeping up alright.

This happened a few more times, spinning to see another group working on moves in the same dancerly ballpark, spinning again and there's another, until it was like a musical or something, all these people coming out of the woodwork to work on their moves, but it was really more like I was just coming out of the woodwork to notice how many people there were working on their moves, very similar to mine, and though we were not with each other, we were dancing together, and I am saying what maybe doesn't need saying: sometimes a dream is also a sign.

(Oct. 18)

23. Sweet Potato Harvest

LAST NIGHT WAS the first freeze, a light one, but it only takes a light one to begin the change amongst the squash, beans, peppers, tomatoes, okra, ground cherries, sweet potatoes, most of the flowers, and a few other things, too. I walked out this morning past the shimmery upright collards and kale leaves and purple osaka mustards, all of them perked up and sweetening up from the kiss of frost, but just beyond them were the slumped squash leaves, big and kaput. Oh, they did a beautiful job this year, made so much fruit, tussled valiantly with the vine borer, played nice with all the other critters sharing the bed. I'm so proud of you, lil butternut. I'm so grateful. And the tithonia, my god, you have given us all so much. Rest now, tithonia. Goodbye for now, basil. Goodbye for now, cherry tomatoes, I know you'll be back. Goodbye, ground cherries. Goodbye, peppers, but let me pull you up and hang you upside down to ripen some more. Marigolds and zinnias and sunflowers and castor beans, goodbye for now, and thank you. And pineapple sage, you did so good, goodbye for now. I and the hummingbirds thank you. And goodbye, sweet potatoes.

Which also means hello, sweet potatoes, the vines of which—though they, too, are starting to wilt, decomposing as we speak—have grown to fill and spill over the eight-by-four raised bed. They are so rambunctious they climb the trellises on two sides. These guys have been working! It has been such a gift to see them thriving even on the hottest days, nary a bead of sweat on their lush brows, which from time to time I will harvest and fry up with some garlic. I gathered up the gorgeous thickets of greenery, kind of like hair, which would make the roots below—*if* there were roots; part of the mystery, the wonder, is that you never really know until harvest—the brains. (That metaphor is wonky, and I'll leave it in for when you need an example of a wonky metaphor.) After I removed the greens, I started rooting around for the roots, plunging my gloved hands—it was cold enough that I was breaking my rule to never garden with gloves on; the soil enters our bodies not only through our mouths, but through the mouths on our hands—into the soil, which yielded a few tubers (these ones, creamy white), but the truth is there are eyes on our hands, too, so I took off my gloves despite the cold, and oh, it was marvelous down there.

So much rip-roaring life: tangles of roots, beetles, and worms; chunks of wood we threw into the bed, when we made it three years back, to hold moisture and break down into soil. And sweet potatoes galore. They were mostly coming in clusters of five and six, often snuggled together like a fluffle of bunnies. A fluffle of purple bunnies snuggled in their dens, because this bed is planted in a purple Hawaiian variety. It didn't take me very long to fill up a five-gallon bucket with tubers, especially because, in addition to the sweet-potato-sized sweet potatoes, I pulled out about four or five the size of my forearm. Luminous purple sweet potatoes the size of my arm, I'm telling you. And after I'd harvested most of the crop, and was finishing up, looking for the little straggling guys hiding in the depths, I noticed myself, I mean *I caught myself*, elbow deep in the earth as I was, really smiling.

(Nov. 3)

24. Squirrel in a Pumpkin

ON A PORCH, down the block, on my way, distracted from which, *reminded of which*, and I was very still so the critter gobbled away though with an eye on me, which you could tell was *really* on me when looking down into the pumpkin for more goodies, looking at me, then looking down, then looking at me, then looking down, then looking at me one more time to be sure I guess I was not actually one of the neighborhood cats dressed up like a human being with a backpack, before plunging headlong into the gourd so that all that remained visible of the critter was that plump butt, those long-footed rear legs, and that tail, buoyant, flamboyant, and well, *gaudy*, even *gauche*, truth be told. Until popping back out of the pumpkin, eyeballing me again while working over this seed, which, to the squirrel, from the looks of it, would be like me eating a little pizza. I'm talking scale here. This squirrel was in the plumping phase of the year, not worried about spring break.

And because of my job, a lucky job as far as they go, I thought, *Oh, this is a delight, let me write this down.* So I elegantly swiveled my backpack into my frontpack, unzipped slowly as possible, reached into the bag, and as I was pulling out my notebook, the squirrel looked at me like *Oh no you don't you cat dressed as a human*, and tipped away, as they do, which might be a small but useful lesson on the differences, or perhaps the consequences, of acquiring, versus being with, or in, or of, the delight.

(Nov. 10)

25. Blue-Spectacle Tulips Hearty to Zone 4

I GUESS I love handwritten notes, I'm thinking, noticing that the bookmark tucked a couple years back into Anna Tsing's book *The Mushroom at the End of the World*, which I'm rereading, is a slip of paper the approximate size of an index card that has handwritten on it: *blue-spectacled tulips hearty to zone* 4. I do not remember where this note comes from, nor from whom, though it is possible that because I am a very lucky person someone gave me some tulips, and this note, too. It's also possible I bought the tulips and they came with the note, though because the note is handwritten it probably would've been some kind of human-scale transaction, which, too, is lucky. The script on the paper, which is, incidentally, a hearty durable paper weathered into a feltish strip, reminds me of my friend

Walt's handwriting, a little bit zany, lots of sharp angles and elbows. (Do you, too, go around feeling love for artifacts that remind you of your beloveds?)

I also have a note dangling from the shelves next to my bed, hand-scrawled on card stock, sent by someone from the Middlebury (Vermont) Natural Foods Co-op (I mean I met her there; she worked there; I don't think she was born there or lived there) who came to a reading I gave at the Bread Loaf Writer's Conference, and after a nice conversation decided to share with me some of her irises, which bloomed this year and good lord. Her notes give description and provenance—what the flowers are called, what they look like, who gave them to her, and when—in a cursive script dating from back when they really taught cursive.

And pinned to a bulletin board—I am 100 percent a bulletin board guy, I understand we are a type; I wonder, is a bulletin board guy more likely to be a hang-onto-notes guy?—is a piece of brown craft paper torn into an approximately eight-by-four-inch rectangle with the word *Truly* outlined in black Magic Marker, in-lined with pink crayon. Actually, it's all caps: TRULY. I found that note between a car's tire and a curb in Newark, NJ, where I was reading at the Dodge Poetry Festival in 2019. That was the year I told the poet Mary Ruefle how much her work means to me by saying, *I kind of copied you, thanks.* Then I spent a dumb amount of time worrying if that was a dumb thing to say, which probably it was. But the most exciting thing about that festival, though it was also a real bummer for the organizers and everyone who traveled to read and listen and the vendors and probably fifty other groups of people I'm neglecting to acknowledge, was that the lights went out. Not just in a venue, but in that whole neighborhood. Some huge underground zap that blew some manhole covers off but thankfully, I'm pretty sure, hurt no one. It was so strange, and sort of wonderful. (Duh: I hope who was on respirators or oxygen tanks, etc., was okay. Duh.)

Oh, aside: at this festival they have a day for the high school children, who descend upon it from all over the Northeast, four thousand kids, which is magic, I have to tell you. Most of those kids were in the symphony hall—which makes it the largest audience I'd read to by far—when I was part of a group reading and made the choice to read, although it was a poetry festival, I guess I was being naughty, a couple short essays, one of which is called "Cocobaby." Though that essay is about trying to regard yourself, and consequently love yourself, with the same tenderness you would a child, these kids only heard, first, the word *testicles*—at which a few screamed out, kind of pleadingly, *yo*! and *hold up!*—and then, when the word *testicles* came out again—*c'mon!* and *easy!* and *trigger warning please!*—and then when I said *penis*, because I can paint a picture, there was audible retching.

The reason I rescued the TRULY note from the street and put it in my bag and carried it home and pinned it to my bulletin board, where it is now, is because I had an Aunt Truly, who we mostly called T, though if I could call after her again I'd say *Truly*, because it's one of the prettier names I've ever heard. My impression is that, of my father's family, Truly was the most inviting to my mother. Truly looked out for her, helped her with us kids, had us for dinner. When my mom set me on the counter for a second and turned her back to stir the gruel or whatever you cook for babies and I fell off the counter onto my head (she's to blame for all these digressions), she called Truly, sobbing and panicked that she'd dropped little Rossy on his head. After Truly talked my mom through checking for bleeding and making sure my eyes could focus through the tears, she said something like *welcome to the club*. And when my mother went along with everyone onto my Uncle Bennet's boat on July 31, 1974, climbing in with her sundress and huge belly—which she could do because, as my Uncle Bennett puts it, *she was an ol' country gal*—and ate copious amounts of fried chicken and potato salad and corn on the cob, feeling rather far away from labor, Truly told her, as she and my father and brother were getting ready to leave, *Girl, you're gonna have that baby tonight*. My mom laughed and said I don't think so. And a few hours later her water broke.

(Nov. 11)

26. Snoopy

DEAR READER, LEST you are under the impression that your humble guide is always delighted, let alone some kind of sage of delight, I need to tell you, I am not. As evidenced by plenty of things, though today it was the feeling—visceral, subcutaneous, vascular, organical, metacarpal, cellular—of annoyance; no, disgust; no, despair—anti-delight supremo—on account of the Macy's Day Parade playing on the television here at my mother's place, where I am staying for the better part of a week, so glad to be with my mom I will endure even this, though my eyes and soul are bleeding some.

She's working on her pies and stuffing in the kitchen, which, when she hears something particularly appealing—which to me is, good bet, something particularly appalling—she takes a quick break, holding her hands a little greasy or crumby in front of her, her head just forward on her little neck, smiling at the horror on the television, which I am using every single ounce of strength not to tell her is a horror, a miserable advertisement for global corporate dominion and nothing more, a big vial of propagandistic poison lubricating us for further submission to the shit show, which she probably knows, or maybe. Or doesn't care, she's got pies to bake. You gotta give it to Macy's and the overlords, those balloons are enticing. They even put a colored in the Rockettes. I can hear through my headphones, inside of which Ricky Lee Jones is trying to soothe my homicidal ideations—homicidal to the TV I mean; homicidal to Macy's—something about a TikTok star so-and-so. He's on a float lip-synching. I wonder what it feels like, pretty bad I bet, until they hand you the check, if they do. I remember seeing my heroes De La Soul in that parade a few years ago, it was a knife in my heart, until I thought, oh yeah, they probably have to pay for medicine and kids and stuff.

Today the way I slipped, trying to ruin the illusion—it is really a pathological immaturity that is most churned up around my mother, I have to say—I told her about the little crew of thieves who used to steal from Macy's at the mall near where we grew up. I wasn't part of that crew, but some of my besties were, one of whom my mother adores, he's a doctor, he'll save your life. I'm pretty sure I was the beneficiary of the larceny, because though they mostly stole in their own sizes, periodically they'd get some huskier gear, and it would come my way. They eventually got busted, but not caught, for no security guard in the Continental is as fast as a thirteen-year-old committed to beating it out of there. *Oh, that's terrible,* she said. (I'm not sure if she meant that the thieving started, or that it had to stop.) Then, when Joe Biden called in to Al Roker, Macy's is on Biden's Board of Directors after all, or Disney is, or whatever thieving consortium of corporations this parade is an advertisement for is—I'm in a state, can you tell? My hackles aflare, you got that?—and my mother, still a romantic per the office of the presidency, reported where the current president was stationed, she keeps up, on Nantucket or something, just down the ocean from the Obamas, who, I blurted out, are worth something like $100 million. I didn't say how many people are sleeping under bridges today. *How do you get that rich*, I asked, meaning to impugn, and my mother, a ninja really, smiled and said *wow, and to think they come from almost nothing*, before turning back to the stuffing, I suspect with her belief in upward mobility and hard work and equality and hope and change affirmed.

It wasn't twelve hours earlier she told me about the day I was released from the hospital for a bout of asthma that lasted four or five days, when the water pump on their car, already held together with duct tape and thread and a couple bungee cords, busted as my mother was picking me up after work. When she parked, she said she saw water running from beneath the hood. After I was wheeled out, she found the pay phone and called a friend who, *thank god* she said, was home. The next day my father walked the four and a half miles from our apartment up to the hospital carrying two five-gallon buckets of water to fill the pump enough to get it home, where he'd replace it, which he would have needed to do promptly, because he would have probably had work later that day down in Philly. Or maybe he drove it over to Pep Boys, I'm not sure.

That was my dad walking on the side of the road with those buckets and no, I don't know why he didn't just carry the empty buckets and ask to fill them at the hospital, but I can speculate a few things, perhaps to do with being black in a white area, perhaps to do with being ashamed to ask, perhaps to do with being afraid. This doesn't delight me. It makes me enraged, I sometimes can't put it down, especially, and this is a puzzle, when my mother, who lived through it more acutely than I did, lived through it most of her life in fact, is on the chair across the room smiling and nodding and talking a little bit to herself in admiration of the Snoopy balloon. *It's so big*, she says. And does a little jig when the next marching band comes on.

I don't need to tell you, the happiest people among us enjoy everything. My mother is not quite among them, she's abundantly irkable, though when she claps and *ooh*s at this debaucherous affair the obvious emblem of our imminent doom, it makes me think, sometimes, she's hella closer than me. Because, in case it's not clear, I *adamantly* do not enjoy everything, and therefore am probably not the happiest people among us, despite being often delighted; for instance, although I hate—*oh, don't say hate*; no, that's the word I mean; I mean *hate*—the Snoopy balloon, I am often delighted by Snoopy, particularly in *A Boy Named Charlie Brown* when Linus kindly gives his blanket to Charlie Brown for good luck on the spelling bee, but is eventually so besieged with delirium tremens that he boards the bus into the Big City, where Charlie Brown is, to retrieve it. He has to take the edge off, dude's gonna have a heart attack. When Linus knocks on Charlie's hotel room door (in the olden days parents were less helicoptery), Charlie and Snoopy see the state he's in—he keeps fainting, the stars keep swirling around his head—and get him in the room. Snoopy, dutiful lieutenant, immediately retrieves a glass of water from the kitchenette, sprinting back to Linus, and then chugs it himself. I think he wipes his mouth by dragging the back of his forearm and hand across it in that cartoon way. He exhales, quenched. Then he does this a couple more times, enough times that—well done, Charles Schultz—we get revved in anticipation: Is he gonna do it again, is he gonna do it again?

He did it again!!!

(Nov. 25)

27. One Million Kisses

YOU MIGHT NOT have pegged me as such, but I used to be the kind of guy, I'm sorry to admit, who did not much truck with little dogs, either in theory or practice, despite being related to one (Stephanie's dog is small) for over a decade. And though I love Tucker, I have not always liked him. It seems mutual—love, occasional dislike, very occasional snapping when I get between him and his mother—some of which perhaps comes from me not liking the idea or the fact of small dogs, which he is, and which a dog can smell on you, and might poop where you're going to step, to let you know. Which makes it a lovely surprise that there is this pipsqueak pup—much smaller even than Tucker—sitting on my lap as I write this, who has been my companion this week as his mother (Stephanie's mother, Myrna) is gone, and has even slept under the covers with me. This morning, coming out from his den down near my knees where he was snuggled into a little moon, he put his two hands on my chest and looked all the way through my eyes into my previously ice-cold-to-his-likes heart, which made it start melting, first thing in the morning, too.

This friendship with Noah the dog encourages me to get on my hands and knees, to his level, at which he then gets even lower, reaching his legs out in front of him and looking up at me, waiting, and when I reach to kiss him, he tilts his face up, and then he jumps back and turns a little circle or chirps before coming back to me and stretching and looking again up at me. It is really something, I can do this for a long time. Sometimes, when I get down on my hands and knees to join him, and maybe growl a little bit or make funny noises, not quite baby talk—puppy talk, I guess—Noah will sidle up next to me (I'm on all fours now, a big dog, kind of a mastiff with smaller teeth, the kind of dog I used to like most of all, now I see), putting his flank against my arm, and kind of lower his head to look at me sideways, which I'm interpreting is his way of saying you are my friend and my mother, which is a reasonable assessment given as in the time it's taken him to do this, I have probably kissed him 8,000 times. I mean I have never kissed a creature so many times, and I have loved and kissed many creatures many times, believe me.

The night before I was to go back home, after he realized I was more interested in cooking myself dinner than playing with him, he disappeared into the living room where, when I went to check on him, I saw that he had snuggled into my winter vest such that his head was peeking out of the armhole. This motherfucker. I let my beans burn while I bestowed upon him a couple hundred more kisses.

When we were taking our final walk, I was hearing some pretty sad music in my head, getting pre-choked up, or whatever that feeling of sadness is that is actually the anticipation of sadness—anticipatory sadness, heads up for that, it'll smash the moment—as he sniffed and peed on every low-to-the-ground thing he could get to, and took a few quick steps toward every squirrel taunting him before looking at me like, *Not gonna happen, huh?* And me at him, *Nah, not gonna happen.* We admired how the last of the leaves falling from the maples lining the towpath were gold, and how they made for us a golden way. We noticed how most everything had died back, and I told him that in a couple months the first sprigs of ferns and nettle will be back. It happens like this again and again, this going and coming, I said, because he's a puppy, and doesn't know what the hell's going on.

That's wild, he said.

You won't believe it, said I.

As I was packing up the car to leave he kept doing his arms-out stretchy thing to get me to be a mastiff, which I did, three or four times, each time kissing him a few hundred times, until the last time, when I said, *I gotta hit it man, I have a long drive, I'll see you soon.* But because he's a puppy, *soon* means little to him. So he stood there, kind of duck-footed like James Harden after a big play, his eyes the biggest in the world, wondering, I think, how long *soon* was, and was it true.

(Nov. 29)

28. Honey Buns

AMONG THE NUGGETS I hang on to and adore—strange, that's how it came out—from Maggie Nelson's book *The Argonauts*, which goes in my satchel of favorite books, of books I will probably reread every few years until I die, is her figuring out that no small part of her job as a mother is tending to her child's asshole. I'm not sure if you call a baby's asshole an asshole, which might make me an asshole, but all the same. It is the parent's duty, in her case the mother's duty, to take care of that precious, indispensable orifice. (I'm not sure if Winnicott put it this way, but good enough parents are really good enough orifice tenders.) The way I've heard it spoken of by the tenders, even if the assholes they speak of may now belong to grown people, is something like their *cute little asshole*. Or *butt* maybe they say.

My mother, a good enough mother by far, to this day often calls me Honey Buns, which, given not only that I am forty-seven years old, but that I was an unequivocal asshole from ages twelve until like two weeks ago, seems to be a reminder, to herself I suspect and no one else, that I once was followed around by a cute little asshole. It's like how parents have pictures of their children at their cutest nearby so they remember their cute little assholes when it might be difficult to do so. The pictures, like the name Honey Buns, help to remind the parents of when the little assholes had cute little assholes.

Long story short: my mother, bless her soul, has not yet retired from her job of caring for my once—*once*—cute little asshole, which persistence might explain why I have a thing with some people being all up in my shit. Which sometimes—I've been told—doesn't mean hovering or prying or bugging me or whatever, but just means giving a shit for your shit, not figuratively, as she reminded me again today over the phone that since I'm almost fifty I better get my colonoscopy scheduled.

(Dec. 2)

29. Lyrica

MAYBE IT'S BECAUSE I'm kind of a words guy, and also a names guy, that when I was doing some undelightful and completely unsanctioned research about pharmaceutical companies, my ears perked up a little extra at the Justice Department's 2009 announcement of the *Largest Health Care Fraud Settlement in Its History*, which was ruled and levied against Pfizer to the tune of $2.3 billion, about $1 billion of which is a criminal fine, in part because they were incentivizing health-care providers (this means taking them on cruises or golf trips or super nice buffets, pretty sure) to prescribe their drugs for uses that the FDA specifically declined to approve. If you were a person and did this—oh wait, corporations *are* people, aren't they?—you'd be prohibited from voting in several states, to say nothing of being allowed to more or less to write the laws, but, I know, I know, I'm probably being hysterical. I just need a pill. Anyhow, probably because I do not often of my own volition watch television—the exception being college basketball whenever and wherever I can get it—and therefore am not compelled by every third commercial to ask my doctor if I should try *x*, *y* or *z*, sometimes without even saying what *x*, *y* or *z* treats, I might be a little bit less fluent in the names of medications, and consequently a little more susceptible to flabbergastment, or gobsmackery—a couple of the many mothers of delight—upon hearing them.

The first three of the convicted four are called Bextra, Geodon, and Zyvox, which I love in no small part because these medications sound like diseases. Or like laundry detergents from the seventies. I have to tell you, you'd have to do some real good convincing to get me to take a pill called Zyvox or Geodon, even if I had any of the way too many conditions they were prescribed not really to treat. But the fourth of the convicted medications especially delights me, and it gives some credence to the almost-refrain among older poets when I was coming up that all the best minds of their generation (aside from their own) had been coopted by ad agencies and other bullshit factories corrupting the language. It's called, I swear to you, Lyrica.

Lyrica's on-label use is as an antiepileptic, a condition some of our greatest writers (Dostoyevsky, some others) suffered from, which, depending on how willing you are to trade Dostoyevsky's and some others' suffering for their books, might dis-recommend the drug. Though I can't really speak to the suffering, for I luckily am not some of our greatest writers, which they found out when I was tested for the condition by a neurologist when I was about sixteen and had begun puking once or twice a day for what seemed like no good reason but was actually a very good reason: as the old people say, *nerves*. In addition to scraping the soles of my extremely ticklish feet with what looked like the same tool with which they unbroke (which means *rebroke*) my nose, putting lots of lights in my eyes and some stuff I cannot remember,[1] they also stuck probes up my nostrils and

---

1 One of the (in my opinion) wonderful conditions, or *diseases*, of the poet, which bleeds into these essays (and which Lyrica might be prescribed to treat!), is to make a few things so personal, so labyrinthine, as to be completely out of reach for most readers. I'm doing that here by very lightly alluding to the tool Tommy Lee Jones and Will Smith use in *Men in Black* to eliminate the memory of people who've seen too much about interplanetary visitors and such, and so instead of killing them like the mob or a government might, they just pull out this tool, which looks like the steel pens my dad used or a tire pressure gauge, trick the person into looking at it, then poof, a light happens that makes them forget. Except when I reference that scene I am never actually referencing that scene, but instead referencing a reference to it, specifically a review of my second book of poems, when I was but a wee poet, wherein the reviewer, referring to my sometimes-purple language

deep into my brain and found *nothing*, which explained for my folks all those C's and sometimes D's I was getting on my report cards, for which afflictions (the puking and the shitty grades), somewhere, Lyrica was probably being prescribed.

Among the most obvious lyrical applications of Lyrica—I mean if I was the one paying people to prescribe it for no good reason, and getting paid to do it—would be for writer's block, a condition I have spent years pretending (and often pretending to the young people who asked me how I dealt with it) I did not deal with, which I did, *every single time* I had an assignment, which is how a lot of these young people have to write: on assignment. (One of the sorrows of teaching school is giving young people assignments rather than invitations.) It was a little bit boastful how I pretended—I wrote in other forms, I wrote letters, I drew, I worked on the other projects I was thinking about—except the truth is, I wasn't pretending: I forgot I, too, got writer's block until someone asked near to when I had an assignment, which I was tearing my hair out about. Anyway, yes,

---

(I didn't know what that meant then; it means over-the-top gooey, not sure where the purple comes from), fair enough seems to me, used as an example a line or two from a sexy poem wherein describing the way in love the world seems to study you, to lean closer to you, including the flowers and their "shivering labia," lines for which, he said, he wished he had that tool.

for writer's block (and writing assignments), try Lyrica. And for the opposite, too—overproduction, writerly diarrhea, hypergraphia (the technical term), evidence sometimes not only of a bounty of questions and an ample stash of beckoning notebooks, but pathological neediness—Lyrica can help. Ask your doctor. (Maybe I should ask *my* doctor.) And for the condition that often overlaps with or is occasioned by writer's block and writer's flood—terrible writing—Lyrica, too, might do the trick.

Though for the sometimes result (depression, anxiety, self-loathing, etc.) of any of the aforementioned writerly maladies, Lyrica should absolutely not be administered, given that suicidal ideations are among its side effects, and you know how poets can be.

(Dec. 4)

30. Vernacular Driving

TODAY I WAS driving from our house in Bloomington to the gym on campus, and at the top of our street I made a right onto a wrong way, before banging a quick left onto Belton Way, a dogleg it's called, I guess in honor of the crookedness of dogs' legs, which I've never really noticed before. This is illegal, I mean "illegal," driving down a one-way and all, though it is part of a vehicular vernacular about which I thought, as I was doing it—and seeing down the road a car coming head on, the driver perhaps thinking, *What the hell*, but perhaps, if they're a local, instead knowing what's going on—*Oh, I love this. It's one of the things we from around here do.*

There are other vehicular vernaculars I love—mind you, I love the vernacular, period: speech, architecture, clothing, cooking, dancing—for instance, that stop sign everyone rolls through, it's really a slow-down sign, you know the one, it is in your neighborhood, too. Or if not that, a yield sign that really means stop. Parallel parking on the "wrong" side of the street, I love it. Or my favorite, which is in deep South Philadelphia on the wider avenues down near the stadium. Like Oregon Ave. for instance, where my friends and I would go to Tony Luke's to get chicken cutlet or roast pork sandwiches, or their famous Uncle Mike's—broccoli rabe, spinach, long-hots, onions, gravy (tomato sauce)—and fries. Where, if you do not hop to when your order is called, they will yell your name so loud you'll pee in your pants a little and cower and apologize as you retrieve the food not for nothing you just paid not nothing for.

The first time we went down there to get sandwiches and be yelled at, we noticed all these cars parked in the middle of the street, what in the rest of the universe would be called a turning lane. It was like another country, another world. *What kinds of savages are these?*, I surely thought, like Kurtz (a character in Conrad's *Heart of Darkness,* a book I have not read, and have been told I should not, which these days inclines me to read it to see why I shouldn't read it). Until I ate their delicious food. But still, the parking made absolutely no sense, it was batshit, who comes up with such a parking strategy? Where'd they learn this outrageous shit?

(Can I pause to tell you, it just flew into my mind, that a buddy of mine whose name I will withhold lest he be retroactively prosecuted, who was the single most parking/traffic/toll-violation–ticketed individual I have ever known, became the parking czar of a major city so he could park where he wanted—often on curbs—without being ticketed? Kids! Pay attention! Follow your dreams!)

But when I went to Italy for a month in graduate school, shortly after first voyaging down there into the South Philly wilds, where the sandwiches were good and the parking bizarre, and wouldn't you know, shortly after arriving in Roma I noticed, in addition to the mopeds, smog, old stuff, watermelon carts open late into the night (they squeeze a little lemon on theirs), and daily interactions with almost incomprehensibly beautiful art and architecture, these people, evidently bananas, too, parked in the middle of the street. And the cars here were petite, so there were more of them. And isn't it something, once you see the origins of the lunacy, once you meet lunacy's folks, the lunacy—parking in the middle of the street; wrong-way doglegs—ceases being lunacy and becomes, instead, tradition, or vernacular. It becomes *This is how we do it here.*

(Dec. 8)

31. As Is My Mother's Way Sometimes

AS IS MY mother's way sometimes, she offered this dime of wisdom as we were driving home from a sweet Christmas at my brother's, almost in passing, dipping into a serious or serious-ish conversation, *grave* maybe is the better word, as is common for us, when she said—describing her grandchildren, now sixteen and fourteen years old, who will forevermore call her Munga, which was precisely how the oldest couldn't say Grandma, both of whom still sometimes like to sleep over, or come over for a meal, and for whom she always bakes a this or a that (that requires some clarification: the best pound cake, eighteen kinds of cookies, etc.), and goes to games major and minor, traveling often quite far to sit on the hard stands despite the arthritis creeping into her lower spine, and worries on their behalf, for she changed their diapers and bathed them and when their parents were off early to work she was the one got them off to school, which included, after waking them up very gently, soothingly as a loon singing their diminutive names, I kid you not, making for them whatever breakfast they wanted, I think they called it *putting in our orders*, usually eggs and bacon for the one, and chocolate chip pancakes for the other, and who still not infrequently takes them to doctor's appointments and always makes the awards ceremonies and the concerts, and if ever their folks are caught up she's the one takes over—*They saved my life. They gave me a reason to stay alive*. She meant after her husband, our father, their (would-be) grandfather, died, and though I was a little bit chagrined to know I was not enough to keep my Dear Ol' Ma tethered to this side, nor my brother, I was glad for whatever got the job done, and how nice it's these two cool kids, inclined to laughter and kindness and keeping an eye on my mother now, too. Though it's not quite how she said it, she meant that she needed to be needed, as we do—I mean, good lord, *we really do*—shy as we are sometimes to acknowledge it, let alone say it. Let alone figure out how to nourish that need. But the grandkids, Hannah and Mikayla, I told you they were cool, came here all needy and sweet to meet for her that need.

(Dec. 25)

32. Goodbye Nana

WE'RE SPENDING A little time in Frenchtown, New Jersey, helping Stephanie's mother, Myrna, as she recovers from hip replacement surgery, for which, if he wasn't so goddamn cute, we'd blame Noah the Dog, who bolted hard after a squirrel while Myrna was walking him a few nights ago, yanking her into the hospital. After I was walking the cute little brute this morning, my phone, which mostly doesn't work in this town, got a brief flash of bars, during which it delivered to me the message from my brother: *Sad News. Nana Died.*

The last time I saw my nana was in October of 2019, when I was reading at a big church in Youngstown, Ohio, where much of my father's side of the family lives, and where I was born. About fifteen minutes before the reading was to begin, in comes a train of my family, a mostly elderly train, and when they walked in that church, it felt like they were bringing with them thousands and thousands of us. As they were walking in, someone alerted me that my Uncle Roy and Nana were out back. My uncle had come all the way from Philly for this reading, swinging up to Cleveland to get Nana on the way, and had brought her here, which, given as his back has been kicking his ass, and his mother could no longer really walk, and other things, was a labor of love.

My uncle brought the hybrid wheelchair/walker contraption to her side of the car, helped her out, there was a brief, frightening moment of teetering, and then she dropped into her vehicle, exhaling with a giggle, and I wheeled her into the church. She was facing me, riding backward, smiling up at me, toothless now, like a child. She told me she was mad at me, for who knows what, and when I gave her a for-who-knows-what face, which involved a grandsonly grin, she got over it and smiled some more. After I stationed her midway back in the church with the rest of the family, I returned to the pulpit, where I read, and was as vulgar as I cannot help but be, about which my nana—a deeply religious woman who will preach your ear off believe you me, if she spots a crack you'll get you some Jesus, some Lord—gave no shits. Nana's into the Lord, not fussing about naughty words.

The family went to Perkins afterward, and Nana, schooled in churchical performance and with an eye and ear for the craft of the sermon, which the reading is a version of, smiled over her menu and said, *Rossy, you had them wrapped around your finger.* She laughed in that wispy way when I smiled and said *thank you Nana*, and then she said, as she often did when delighted, *lordhamercy.* My uncle Roy showed me eight thosand pictures of his new grandbaby—pictures that all seemed like the same picture to me, but the baby's not my grandbaby—and Nana and her sister Butter jawed at each other about who worked harder at their mother Biggie's barbershop, a version of the same fight I bet they've been having for almost a century. Butter throws verbal knives without looking up from her menu, but after Nana's chucked hers, she looks around and laughs and makes eyes like *You hear me?*

My nana was a certain kind of difficult person who had been forged in varieties of difficulty. She struggled, maybe you'd call it, with mental health stuff, in ways I've often felt close to. So close that for a spell and desperate for an explanation or source to my troubles, and reading the books and the websites, I thought, *Oh, it skips a generation; that's gonna be me.* She put her home phone, rotary, in her purse, is what I'm saying. She once slashed up her furniture with a knife so no one would take it and smashed up all the china my folks sent her when they were in Guam. Though who knows my father's troubles, the ones he tamped down by working and drinking, he seems mostly to have taken those with him to the grave.

All of which is to say, maybe after it got me, I just got it, and I more kind of got her. Hers was a universe running parallel to ours, and periodically the two lined up, like when I'd be driving her down to see my father, who was dying in a hospital called Mercy, who was soon to become her second dead son, and a song might come on, let it be Marvin Gaye, let it be Al Green, and we'd sing it together, and she'd laugh and say *Alright Rossy.* Or two Christmases ago, when I was at my mother's and we called and got to talking about her meal, what she cooked herself, and when she got to the cornbread, I asked, *How'd you learn it, Nana?* She said *Momma*, almost like, *Where else would I have learned it?*, and when I asked if she measures, she said, *No no, I make it the old way. We just know.*

This delight has an odd shape and feel I am realizing, and maybe that is because it is an elegy, a goodbye I will surely be working on until I follow her out of here. Which reminds me of two things: the way she said my name, the first syllable open and soft like a saucer or a pool, like a warm bath in the middle of a garden.

The second syllable she lilted up, like a bird shaking jewels of water from her before lifting from that bath. That's what my nana sounded like sometimes. And if she didn't call me Rossy, she called me Baby, like when we last got off the phone, and I said, *I love you, Nana*, and she said, *I love you too, Baby*, and then, for emphasis, *Mm-hmm*.

(Jan. 10)

33. Unusual Mailbox

IT IS UNUSUAL a mailbox chokes you up, and because there are too many probable causes—not for the mailbox: for my being choked up—let me simply tell you it was the phrase affixed in those janky silver sticker letters, usually used for a name or address, a little crooked, the *V* and the *W* peeling slightly, the phrase itself leaning back, lounging, or maybe almost indiscernibly ascending:

TRAVELERS WELCOME

(Jan. 12)

34. Boom: Here's Loo

PERHAPS IT IS that smell and memory are snuggled up in the same nook/culvert of the brain, and that I have, at forty-seven and change, in all likelihood, summited the midpoint of my life, or plumbed it, or zipped by it, or it has happened—without that midpoint even having the common courtesy to ring a bell or *jolly good fellow* me—that scents, as I get older, become more powerful. I don't mean I smell more acutely (which I do, it seems, every day, since I broke my nose at Veteran's Park in Langhorne, Pennsylvania, summer of 1998, remind me to tell you that one; after the whack I played another two hours and when coming home to my mother's she said of my now firmly set and crooked sniffer, *Oh, Rossy, your nose*, because she not unreasonably probably somewhat thinks of it as her nose), I mean the emotional heft or register of scent is more likely these days to make me stop whatever I'm doing and look around for the origin of that scent, which is the origin of the often palpable emotional experience I am having at that moment, which is why the looking tends often to be as much inside as out, into the vault or repository or library or however you want to think of it where, for better or worse, there are more memories of scents stored than I will have a chance to make with the days I have left.

None of which I was thinking when we went to see our friend Loo at her studio today, which, the second we walked in, I recognized by its scent, which is, I suppose, a blend of some machinery, book-making supplies, fabric, knickknacks, and probably a handful of cigarettes a day, a handful and change when she's working really hard, I bet. Probably her shampoo or soap some, too, the smell of her body some, too. Whether we were coming to see her or not, the experience, the recognition, would have been the same. Boom: here's Loo. The comfort, the a-ha, the *delight*, was in recognizing, and *recognizing I was recognizing*, the smell of someone I love, or the smell that reminds me of a person I love.

My mother's hand lotion, and castile soap, will never not remind me of her. If I smell the cologne Colors (De Benetton for Men), there's my brother, and whiplashingly so. My dad was Right Guard Fresh mixed with whatever restaurant he was working in, especially when the deodorant was wearing off and his body came through, a scent I replicated almost exactly (sans the restaurant) in my twenties. My friend Gerald Stern smells of wool. My grandfather wore a hair cream, and I guarantee if someone walked by at this moment wearing it, after wondering why that person was wearing the hair cream of a hundred-year-old man, I'd say *There goes Grampa.* My nana's is also her hair. How often it is our hair, I'm realizing, from which our scents commence. The smells of former lovers—mostly shampoos; a body oil or two—are powerful with me; former nearly lovers, too.

About twenty years ago a friend of mine in Easton, PA, who worked at a café that smelled of buttery egg-and-cheese sandwiches on bagels and set me up with her daughter (it didn't take, which some people say means we didn't smell good to one another; also, I was more taken with the mom, as I think perhaps the mom was with me and the set-up, as it seems to me so often to be, was an attempt to cuddle [or couple] by proxy) told me, or rather me and all the people eating their bagels and drinking their coffee at the bar and the nearby tables, that one of the sexiest things a man ever did to her was to pick up her scarf, which was long and trailing behind her, and smell it, deeply. (For those of you picturing

Hannibal Lecter, we all know—I mean we adults all know—the difference between the sexy and the creepy, whether it's someone smelling your scarf or licking your ear, is whether or not you want it to happen.) She mimed lifting a scarf to her face, which could've been a bouquet of lilacs or a bowl of soup or someone's scalp, and she inhaled, closing her eyes and smiling a little bit, and then she laughed and pointed at the far-as-I-knew quite shy guy sitting at the counter who did it, who blushed and smiled and stood up from his stool and took a bow.

(Jan. 15)

35. Gnomes

WHOEVER MAKES IT their business to stick gnomes in the crook of a tree, I love you, I realized today, walking down Fourth Street toward the towpath along the Delaware River, when I looked up from navigating the heaved and hazardous sidewalk (delight, though sometimes costly: the heaving that the roots of trees sometimes cause; i.e., the reminders that trees don't play) and found myself staring directly into the eyes of a kindly old gnome, who was standing in the crook of a tree, waving, or maybe blessing me, or benedicting, or whatever it is gnomes do. Sometimes these people stick—probably not stick; they probably place or arrange or *offer*—gnomes around their gardens or on windowsills or ledges, or they make gnome villages, in my experience usually (but not always) doing so on or along public pedestrian ways, enchanting the heretofore dull path. As far as I gnow, the gnomes have not yet been appropriated into white supremacist mythology and such in the way that I understand the Vikings maybe have—the guys in boats not the football team; too kindly and cute I suppose the gnomes are,[1] but if they have been, forgive me, I didn't know.

Back in the day, when I had the oxblood Dr. Marten boots and traded the black shoelaces for white ones from my basketball kicks—as much as I have professed

---

1 When my brother was five years old, his best friend, Steven, who lived a couple doors down from us in the apartments in Painesville—it's a miracle when something good happens in a place called Painesville, just as it is in Hurtzville or Woeburg or Miserytown or Bummersbury—kicked him in the nuts. When my mother went to confront his mother about the kick, she said, *Well, you know, Mathew's father is kind of, umm, different*, by which she meant black, which, not discounting my poor brother's assaulted little nuts, was kind of a priceless deflection, if that's the word. She was blaming my black dad, or more accurately, my dad's being black, for her son's kick. In other words, she was teaching her son to be white. Or rather, *White*. Anyway, when my mom recounts this story, she always says that my brother said—this she says in a child's disappointed voice; my mother is dramatic, often comically so—*I thought everyone was a Smurf*, referring to the cartoon about a community of mostly benevolent tiny blue gnomish people that my brother and I pretty religiously watched on Saturday mornings, often making a fort by throwing an afghan over a couple chairs to do so. But my brother was kicked in the nuts in the late seventies, and *The Smurfs* was televised between 1981–1989, so it could not have been so, though the point, if anachronistic, is still taken: little Matty, who at the time of the kick was mostly called Meemee, thought everyone was as kindly as a gnome, when in fact, Steven—no no, Steven was a baby with a strong leg . . . It was Steven's mom, that day anyway, who was acting like a Viking.

a kind of antifashion, I have always been trying to be pretty; what a relief to just recognize it, and go all out—my buddy Walt, a little more aware of skinhead symbology than I, asked me ironically, kindly, if I was in the Aryan Front or whatever team was those days wearing that uniform—oxblood Docs with white laces. Regardless, for the time being, I love the gnomes, and the gnome people, and their ilk, which to me includes, among others, the matchbox car people, the bottles (or even sometimes crystal balls) on rebar people, the lots of windchimes people, the million bumper stickers on their van people, the stone frogs in the garden people, the birdhouse people, the weathervane people, and the overboard (tombstones, mechanized vampires, etc.) for Halloween people.

(Jan. 16)

36. OREO Speedwagon

ONE OF THE lovely features of my job, which I've mentioned before and will probably mention again, is the no-longer-quite-infrequent notes I get from folks who have read something I've written—every one of which, if I were a different person, I would respond to, fully and with love, which I do in my heart every single time I receive one of them, I am so grateful—oftentimes, in addition to some personal stuff and a little gratitude, they share with me a delight or two. Seriously! Part of my job is receiving by mail, electronic or post, a delight. (Although I'm not that guy, this is what you might call a life hack.) A quick observation to say that this confirms something I have said before, which is that delight compels us to share. And also to note that these letters, these *delights* I am given—it's a basket of delights, really—are given to me in return—not exchange exactly, more like we're sharing it—for the basket of delights I've given them, all of which had actually been given to me. I think we are getting to the bottom of something, friends! There is a burgeoning theory of the systemic before us, or perhaps the rhizomatic or mycelial or the invasive—ooh, *invasive delight*, that'd make a good T-shirt. Of course, delight as contagion—*epidemic delight*—that's nice, too.

ALL THAT SAID.

I got a note in my school mailbox, handwritten—the handwritten note, the letter, by post, not from a lawyer, among the delights—in a script that reminds me of at least two people I love. Kinda three. This is one of the notes, on a small, unassuming card with a yellow border, where I get a little gratitude (the words THANK YOU in an almost faint gold), and I get a little life detail, which, in this case, is also a delight (this person's coworker has a guinea pig named OREO Speedwagon.) As much as this goes into my basket of delights (and perhaps now yours), the delight I want to share today is that this person, who does not know me, signed off their letter with

Love,

(Jan. 17)

37. Dad in Dream Unaging

OH, THE MANY jewels of aging. (Let me briefly address the persistence of these jewels, verging on the tedium, which perhaps keep glimmering forth because of the chronological, daily, diaristic nature of this book, also maybe because it's a kind of sequel, which, too, makes it an episode, which encourages a particular kind of noticing, and noting, of time's passage. One might even say that though the nominal subject of the book is delight—in addition to attention, language, the mind, memory, relationships, and a few others—the real subject is the passage of time. Time, or time's passage, seems to be what makes the jewels, if that's even the metaphor anymore, sparkle. Or accumulate—like riches: maybe it's that.)

Oh, oh, the many jewels of aging. It has recently come to my attention—I mean, I thought it yesterday when I was playing ball with a bunch of college kids, and here's the thing; I'm a quick jumper, and being such ameliorates one of the ravages of aging, which is that I'm no longer, as I once really was, a very high jumper; but as a quick jumper (this is insider talk, I know) I'm still able to get taps and offensive rebounds and put-backs, which happened the other day, three or four misses I tapped and recovered before putting the ball in, à la Moses Malone, then yelled to B, in the third person (as is my preferred mode of shit talk), *Damn, that dude's almost fifty!*—that that dude's almost fifty. As of writing this, almost exactly forty-seven and a half, or as the kids where I grew up used to say, which even then puzzled me for its obviousness, *forty-seven going on forty-eight.*

There are many interesting things about being a teacher—oh, let me just say *weird*—among them is that the people you're paid to be around, the students, for the most part all stay the same age. Or in an Einsteinian way, relativity I'm talking about, they're getting younger. I hear myself talking sometimes to them, or trying to relate to them, to be *relatable*, as they say, these people who for the most part used to be like my little siblings in age (I started young, in my mid-twenties), and then became like my very little siblings (i.e., surprises; i.e., accidents) in age, and who now are like my children, the undergraduates and the graduate students. Among the evidence, significant because I am a person who cares about, and knows something about, music: I know almost none of their music. Perhaps among the more convincing evidence: when I am introduced to their music, mostly, I decide to keep not knowing it. But it's not only the students getting younger.

Last night I saw my father in my dream, which I do frequently, luckily, and we talked a little bit about the writer John Edgar Wideman. My brother was there, too. My father was admiring Wideman books in the dream, talking about how he was a star ball player in Pittsburgh, just as my dad was in Youngstown. It might be the case that my dad's rebounding record still stands, I guess I ought to look that up. In the dream my dad and I were having an easy time, and he was being neither arrogant nor braggy, which he could suffer from a little bit. Nor was I being surly and judgmental, which I can suffer from a little bit. We were talking and listening to each other and probably touching a little bit. There was a feeling of—oh here it is—*safety*, which, I'm realizing, might be the common feeling of my dreams with my father. The most potent one of all was some years back, when I was on some kind of a military airplane, there were no seats, I was leaning against the interior wall of the plane, and we were being tossed about in a storm that I knew was going to bring the plane down. Until the pilot looked back and he was my father, at which point I knew it'd be okay.

Anyhow, it wasn't until waking up and laying with my eyes closed a while this morning, trying to catch hold of where I'd been, and with whom, as I do most mornings I do not have to get up and go, that I noticed, *I realized*, that in my dreams, my father doesn't look a day older than he was when he died. Which I cannot say for myself.

(Jan. 30)

38. My Neighbor's Face

AS I WAS walking home today, my neighbor pulled up next to me in his car, rolled his window down, and said, very gently, *Hey Ross*, while pointing at our car, which has a crumpled rear end, and the back windshield busted out. It's a mess. He looked alarmed, worried, and concerned, which explains his tone of voice, solemn, soft, pointing from the seat of his car to ours, this dude with whom I suspect I perhaps do not share some values. Hang on. How long can I abide in myself the infantile, arrogant notion that I would know anything about anyone's values without asking them what they value, myself included? I mean to say I bet I didn't vote like my neighbor in 2020—maybe there was a sign or a sticker?—which, if we're being real, might not actually have all that much to do with values; for political parties, and perhaps more explicitly the heads of those parties, do not have values, they have donors, they have shareholders, and they have promises, both parties, which more and more seem like one party, that they have no intention to keep. Oh, I guess I stand corrected: those *are* values.

But per values I would like to share with my neighbor, I *aspire* to share with my neighbor—along with knowing his name, which is sort of step one in being a good neighbor, which places me at step zero, trailing him on that front—let me simply report what he said to me, softly, just as I hope I also would do if I saw my neighbor's car crunched up, making my face as loving and tender as I could, just in case of the worst, as he did, looking over at the wreckage, pointing: *Is she okay?* He didn't mean the car (that would be a difference of values), he meant the most-often driver of the car, Stephanie. We then had a nice laugh about it once it was established all was okay, it was Stephanie's very rubbery twenty-seven-year-old son driving, and he was okay, as was the driver of the truck who rear-ended him. My neighbor exhaled loudly, shaking his head, and said, *Phew, it looked bad.* Then he lauded the Honda, patting the door of the one he was driving, which, though I'd seen him driving it at least one million times, if you were to have asked me earlier, I would've told you, with great conviction, that he drives a Chevy or Ford. And after we were together praising the Honda—me mainly about mileage and how long they seem to run—he said something technical about axles or carburetors or WD-40 or something and I pretended I understood and nodded and laughed and thanked him for checking on us.

(Feb. 1)

39. Scarecrow the World

WALKING HOME YESTERDAY just past the abandoned something-or-other that in five years will be an expensive something-or-other, I noticed a winter glove stuck onto the end of a tree branch, waving to all passersby. I first admired it as a scarecrowish sculpture, and if not exactly a sculpture, then maybe a kind of performance. It is worth noting that one time my buddy Jay and I suspended a deceased carp (we did not decease the carp) from an overpass, high enough it wouldn't slap a windshield but low enough you could see it. Also, when some kid in the neighborhood was messing with his brother—it's possible there was a racial flavor, or we made it so anyway to accommodate the forthcoming—we were going to stuff the groundhog we found on the side of the road into the mailbox where this child lived which, I know, I know. Boys should not be allowed anywhere near *The Godfather* or mailboxes. I have been *my bad*ding about that idea, and thousands of others, for decades, and it is largely from experience—the first person I mean; though it's true we did what we did, it was always by a hair's breadth that we didn't do what we didn't, thank god—that I derive my belief that no child should ever be prosecuted for a crime. Experience and, how do they say all day every day these days, *Trust the science*? I.e., You can see it in the scans, children's brains are like Swiss cheese. Actually, the holes I think stay there deep into their twenties, some of the children. There are all these mice running through their brains.

It is now written: if a child chops me up and feeds me to the piranhas, don't you dare prosecute that child. Get that child help. But let it be known, Child, if I get loose before you chuck me in the tank, I'm gonna fuck you up. Unless you're bigger than me. Or are even just a decent wrestler. Anyway, because, thank god, the groundhog was too big for the mailbox, we just rested the critter at home plate in the diamond they'd chalked into their cul-de-sac. We propped his little chin on a wiffleball we found against the curb. It was a performance. That's why I went down this road, which I think I probably shouldn't have. Anyhow, it took me only a few seconds to realize the engloved tree probably wasn't a performance—there we are; I have been establishing my expertise, offering my bona fides—it was probably someone found the glove and thought that a good way to display it for the poor cold-handed sod who lost it would be at, depending, eye-ish level. Making of the tree a lost and found, which is, if long coming, the delight.

I know, or suspect I know, this is the case (an ad hoc lost and found) because I have seen it before, many times, though until now did not quite realize what I had been seeing. Now I know what it was, and know that, like you, I have done it. Found something someone lost and stuck it someplace they might more easily see it when they come back for it. Someone recently dropped a baggie of cash—don't get excited, it might've been twenty bucks or something—just outside of my studio, which abuts the vegan bakery. My friend Dave and I, walking out of the studio to the bakery—I think it would be negligent of me not to pause to acknowledge the delight of having one's workplace abut the vegan bakery, where the food is good and the people are kind; it would also be negligent not to acknowledge the delight of having at our disposal the word *abut*—spotted the baggie, thought *uh oh*, asked the kind vegan bakery people if they knew who the baggie belonged to, or who it might, which they didn't, so we decided we'd put it right outside my studio door, in fairly plain view, but just barely covered, held down really, with a wooden shingle, which was a strange thing to have found outside of this former industrial building, but whatever. The baggie of cash was very near where it was dropped, but just off the sidewalk, which gave it, I think our thinking went—we just did it, collaboratively, and quickly, without going through it like an essay might—a better chance of sticking around for whoever dropped it and would likely be coming back for it, for baggies of cash are valuable.

It sat there for several days, a baggie of cash outside the studio. I'd laugh every time I came back to the studio, unlocking my door and seeing the baggie still in plain view beneath the shingle. Not infrequently when I was inside the studio, I'd notice someone sort of notice it, turn their heads at it like some dogs do when you talk to them, but leave it be. And one day, maybe two or three weeks later, I saw someone walking her dog spot the baggie of cash, bend over to see if it was what she thought it was (I'm presuming), and (I'm presuming) because she thought someone left it for someone else as an open-air Venmo, and (I'm presuming) because she wanted the transaction to go through, or the money to get where it needed to go, she put the shingle all the way over the baggie of cash.

Man, people do their best. And sometimes it's so good.

(Feb. 2)

40. Michael McDonald

MY INCLINATION—I AM feeling it burbling inside, it's a nervous little guy, skitterish—is to overexplain this one, but let me not—but let me interrupt briefly to adore the grammatical construction, first made familiar to me by my childhood friends Jim and Vrante, *let me not*, or *let me stop*, which is a way of saying I should not do *x* or *y*, a way of acknowledging a transgression while dipping one's toe into it, a way of doing the naughty thing and asking forgiveness later: aside: let me recommend the poet Lyrae Van Clief-Stefanon's meditation on the construction *let me had been*, in her essay "Seeing to Be: Daring the Impossible to Make Each Other Possible," it will blow your mind—and instead tell you that—as we were walking downtown, slipping around and sliding and having fun because ours is a municipality that for some reason does not believe in plowing, at least not plowing well, I mean it is comical and the kind of thing that makes you think I hope they are plowing that unused money into the schools, into the hospitals, the pipes and playgrounds—I heard Michael McDonald's voice approaching, dopplerish, from behind us: *I keep forgettin' we're not in love anymore, I keep forgettin' things will never be the same again.*

If you are me and you hear Michael McDonald's voice approaching overloud from a car in Bloomington, oh you get happy. And extra happy when you realize McDonald's husky, timpanic, surprisingly rangy voice—by which I mean he has range, his highs are pretty high and his lows pretty low, which seems remarkable to me given the particular husky resonances of his voice; his voice is like a timpani mixed with a cello—was being accompanied by the driver of the sedan, I think it was a Buick, whose ears were being somewhat protected from how loud his music was because his doo-ragged head was halfway out the window singing along, I mean he was belting along with Michael McDonald *to the world.*

Yo, it was so goddamned loud, and you might call it profiling, go ahead and call it profiling, but I wasn't surprised in the least it was a brother, not because of the volume, but because of the Michael McDonald, who we love, and no wonder, for he's the one who won't stop singing, against what they keep telling us, *You don't know me but I'm your brother.* *(Feb. 6)*

41. Mistranscription

I HAVE BEEN reading through the transcriptions of these delights this morning, and have been many times confused by a word choice I seem to have made, or some odd spelling that makes no sense in my realm of spelling (or misspelling), and I am reminded that, oh right, many of these delights have been transcribed by my friend Bernardo, to whom, because my handwriting verges on the indecipherable, rather than just giving him the notebooks for him to transcribe himself, we decided I ought to read them to him, and he can type them in. He is Bernardo the Scrivener. He is Bernardoby the Listener and Scrivener, quill-less. And as per working conditions, I think he's paid alright, I feed him food and coffee, and when he puts his laptop on his lap I give him a thick book to put between his work and his family jewels.

Bernardo is not a terrible scrivener, he is not an especially slow typist, but he's not an especially good scrivener either, for he's not an *especially* slow typist. It's plodding work, choppy, stammery, repetitive, inefficient, a poor use of my research money and time, and for those very reasons it is most often pretty fun. The delights foment stories, digressions, make us forget that we're on the clock, which is what they're meant to do. Despite that, given as I can be having fun *and* be somewhat impatient, I encourage Bernardo not to spend time correcting after each essay, which he wants to do, diligent employee he is. It's already a slow-go, so I tell him *leave it be, I'll get it later*, which means sometimes reading over these transcriptions, like this morning, I get to a word or phrase and I am like *what in the hell am I talking about?*

Because I didn't say it. Bernardo heard it, and so scrivened it as though I said it, which, we've established this, I didn't. But sometimes his mishearing is better than what I said—not usually, trust me; usually it's just batshit, like *Dude, I don't think this scrivener thing's gonna work out for you*; but also, for those of you considering hiring this guy for scrivening, it is the case that I am the oft-deployer of the ridiculous neologism, and I'm not always the most enunciative locutioner, laughing as I do at some of my sentences, or humming with admiration, *ooh that's good*, which throws a scrivener off, so cut him some slack, he comes highly recommended!—like this one, from some essays back: " . . . a bit more enamored of the root, which, like every root, is a story." That essay is about riding my bike down Third Street to my studio, and what I see along the way, which makes it odd to transcribe the word *route* as "root." If I was looking to fire Bernardoby, which I would never, I might say *context*, then snatch his quill. Though this homophonous error is less odd once you realize how often I use the word *root*, which one could find by typing it into the search bar. About which abundant usage (I think it's nineteen, as of this revision), I assure you, my editor, always at war against repetition (she might say *overuse* or *a wanting lexicon*) is going to get on me to thesaurus those. We'll see. I guess I might prefer not to.

Anyway, I have veered, as per usual, from the observed delight, which is the delightfully mistranscribed thing, the mistranscribed thing that rattles all the lightbulbs in the chandelier in your head. Bernardoby's mistranscription, his mistake, couples or enswirls or *routes* the path or way into the botanical (roots are avenues or roads, etc.), and makes the act of rooting (à la the botanical, searching in the dark for nutrients; à la pigs, searching for treasure with one's snout or other appendage, often beneath something; and à la what I am doing for Bernardo right now: *cheering*) a story. Short form: roots are stories. We all know roots are resplendently, radically metaphorical, but thanks to Bernardoby's poetic mistranscription, they are to me now even more so.

An essay I frequently teach for this very reason is Patrick Rosal's "The Art of the Mistake," one of the best essays about making poems and art that I know. In it he tells about being with his crew of dancers at a battle in Newark or Jersey City, which is going kind of neck and neck until the worst dancer in their crew, June—delight: that every crew has a worst, whether it's a crew of dancers or a basketball team or quiz bowl team or shoplifters or a choir, and our proclivity is, as we say in basketball, to *hide* that lead-footed motherfucker, which really means to play such that their lead-footedess is less bad (i.e., in hoop we play zone) so we can keep them on the squad, which (the squad) is the only reason to play these games anyway—does a little toprock before unfurling into a suicide, a move in which you do an almost front flip, landing on your back, often with a demeanor of affrontery—arms crossed posing, hand on crotch whatevering.

In this case, June hit his suicide and while turning through the air somehow tossed his unlaced shell-toe Adidas from his foot to his hand and when he landed he tucked the clunky shoe with those wide-ass shoelaces beneath his ear, chilling, like *what now*? Boom, his crew won, and it turns out, he confided later as they were celebrating, asking where he learned that, that it was an accident. He got lucky and caught the kick, which he'd actually meant to tighten up before they started dancing. And he got luckier still when, realizing his kick flew into his hand, he had the wherewithal to slide it mid-air beneath his head and pose like he meant to do it.

(Feb. 8)

42. DeBarge on Tiny Desk

MY FRIEND AIMEE sent me a link to one of those NPR Tiny Desk Concerts, featuring El DeBarge, which, though I am hyperbolic by nature and design, is unhyperbolically one of the most beautiful things I've ever seen. And not only because El looks good, like really good, but that, too. For those of you *black don't crack*-ers out there, El, like your gentle guide, has a lot of cracker in him, first that. But as you *black don't crack*-ers out there will also probably know, El, as far as I understand it, had a string of very difficult years, intense addiction stuff, which can put a beating on your collagen, teeth, brain, and, oh yeah, voice.

My god his voice. El had a silky falsetto as a young man, which makes sense, for the falsetto—at least a certain kind of airless, dense, smooth falsetto—is a young man's game. Listen to Gallant or Moses Sumney. Or better yet, and more to the point, listen to Maxwell's *MTV Unplugged* version of Kate Bush's song "This Woman's Work," which, if you're like me, you'll need to watch—I guess today I listened to it on Youtube, which means I also listened with my eyes—three or four times so you can deal with yourself, put your heart back in your chest and such. Let me not try to describe it. But when he sings it these days, fifteen or twenty years later, though it's still Maxwell, it's a different Maxwell, more nodules, more grit, more air, the latter of which we're all turning into anyway. It's for this reason, among others I'm sure (including how men sometimes are like birds; including how men, sometimes, are girls), that the silky falsetto is so moving to us—it's the glimmering sonic anticipatory evidence that all is change. Which is also to say that Maxwell's voice twenty years later, further along on its voyage to air, is also beautiful, and wordlessly so. (I sometimes think that one of the purposes of the beautiful, by the way, is to leave us, or rather bring us, to wordlessness. To grant us some silence.)

All to say though, and here's the thing, and delight underdoes it: El, in these fifteen minutes, singing "I Know This Love Is Real," a little mash-up of "This Dream" as tribute to Martin Luther King, which rolls into "Love Me In a Special Way," by which time he's donning a Kangol, sounds almost precisely like his seventeen-year-old self, as is confirmed by the comments, the blackest comments I promise you ever left behind one of these little desk concerts, the blackest comments to ever be planted in the gardenia field of NPR. Lots of *give him his flowers* and *where's his lifetime achievement award*. And part of his lifetime achievement might be not only his angelic voice, but his being here with us at all. I mean his being alive.

Some years back I found myself in a DeBarge rabbit hole—if you have to go into a rabbit hole, this is a good one—and it led me from the videos, to some live performances, to some interviews, to, at last, this strange little clip, amateur, maybe someone's shitty phone, of El and Whitney Houston seeing each other, it seems like backstage at some event, or maybe at an after-event or something, maybe some awards show or concert, I'm not really sure. Nor do I know what their relationship was, if it was friends, siblings-ish, rivals, mutual admirers, something else. But what I do know is that when they get to each other through the very thick crowd—which takes some doing, although it feels, too, like the crowd itself is trying to let it happen, they are parting themselves for Whitney and El—they embrace as I've seen people embrace very few times in my life. My father and his brother moments before my dad was wheeled to the surgery that would determine how long he would live. A couple guys outside a hospital in Philly. After a funeral. An airport goodbye or two I've witnessed. Been a part of. I remember thinking it was the kind of embrace you find yourself in when you can't believe the other person is still alive. Or when you know there's a good chance they won't long be. I remember thinking there was an aura around them, some kind of hush, or silence, or light.

And so maybe part of the wonder of this Tiny Desk Concert, by which I mean El and his falsetto, is that it has not only the timbre of escape, or survival, but also that, lifting from his scathed body, this scathed life, it sounds like resurrection. Which wrings me into mind of Aretha Franklin's version of "Mary, Don't You Weep" on her album *Amazing Grace*, where Aretha as Mary wails to Jesus, she kind of accuses him really, that *if you'd've been here, my brother wouldn't have died.* And then Aretha Franklin as Jesus, before she goes to sing Lazarus from that cave, she lets it be known, this is *for the benefit of you who don't believe.*

(Feb. 13)

43. Garlic Sprouting

ALTHOUGH I INFREQUENTLY feel it when I'm planting garlic in the fall, always later than I'm supposed to (ballpark Halloween, in my book), and although this is my thirteenth consecutive year of planting garlic during which I've had twelve either reasonably or exceptionally successful crops, I realized today that I plant garlic, every year, with no small degree of doubt that it will actually come up, or *make*, as we say in the trade. I mean, when it comes to garlic, I am batting 1.000. I should say, garlic is batting 1.000. I just hand garlic the bat. But you get my point. Though I didn't realize, or better yet, I didn't *register*, that I plant garlic doubtfully until today, as I was sitting on the back porch because spring is springing and we're having a warm one, and midway through a phone call I cast my gaze unexpectantly over the garlic beds and, wouldn't you know, they were all sprouting, unsheathing a few hundred green blades up toward the sun. With the enthusiasm of someone witnessing a miracle, Lazarus waltzing from his cave or something, I interrupted the friend I was talking to, *Wait, wait, yo, it's up, it's sprouting! The garlic's sprouting! It's up!* (The friend seemed glad for me.) Who knew that in addition to vampires and getting your tomato sauce right, garlic's your tiny professor of faith, your pungent don of gratitude?

(March 3)

44. Being Read To

IN WHAT WOULD prove to be a somewhat lazy day, a day we would neither seize nor attack nor crush nor murder nor decapitate nor defenestrate but, simply, live, languorously and loungily, Stephanie drinking her tea, me my coffee, in bed and pj's past noon, and in no big hurry to fix that, which makes the puritans in us whirl in their graves, hastening happily their conversion into soil, and worm shit, and flowers. From our sloth Stephanie started reading from Eduardo Galeano's book *Soccer in Sun and Shadow*, which is one of my favorite books and, I think, now hers. It's a kind of history of soccer, f*ú*tbol, told in short essays (essayettes), from Galeano's perspective not only as a pretty hardcore fan but also as one of our most important and searing writers on colonialism and empire. Also, there are drawings.

This is the second or third time we've read Galeano's book, having come to it first stumbling around the public library, *browsing* is the word, wandering, wondering for some guidance on a book of epistolary basketball essays I'm working on with a friend. I'd read (and taught) some of Galeano's *Memory of Fire Trilogy*, and his book of fables *The Book of Embraces*, but I still need to, or should, read his *Open Veins of Latin America*, which I understand is one of the most important books I'll ever read. Per that last sentence, that *should*: how lucky, even if it sometimes pricks you with shame (*should* is one of the cudgels of shame, especially *should have*), even if it has compelled you to pretend to the contrary, not yet to have read even near everything by your favorite authors. Thanks to your having been a shabby and half-assed student, there are so many books to look forward to.

I was reclined with my coffee on my chest as Stephanie flipped back and forth through the book reading essayettes, which, though Galeano's book moves chronologically, it invites. It might be the brevity of the essays, or that they mostly stand alone, or just that reading a book not front to back can be a delight. (I recently realized, reading C. D. Wright's book *Cooling Time: An American Poetry Vigil*, that I really love to read books—maybe especially books of poems, or poem-adjacent stuff—back to front.) Vignettes of famous players; stories of miraculous games; how Brazil became Brazil when they finally started playing their black players, among whom was Pelé. And slightly longer riffs on the World Cups, which Galeano, being Galeano, historicizes, makes events in and of and with the world, never missing a chance to describe, often with comedic flourish, the powers that be, teasing, for instance, that Castro's revolution is any day (this starts in 1962) to be overthrown.

There's also a slight nostalgiac bent to *Soccer in Sun and Shadow*, a longing for the good old days of the game,[1] which seems to me to include a more flamboyant and dancerly manner of play, a game in which form, or style, was as important as function, or winning. A game free of things like owners and corporate sponsorships and everyone and everything branded like cattle—i.e., the general bleak consumptive way of sport, which emerges, hard to remember sometimes, from *play*; the vast, wonderful collaborative unknown, which is, pretty sure, antithetical to capital, and which Galeano,

---

1 Note bene: Although sometimes "the good old days" is code for when women and black people couldn't really vote, etc., sometimes it's really not. Sometimes it means when I liked the soccer (or the pizza or the buildings or the unions or the price of college or the Roe v. Wade) more.

a romantic with a fierce memory, dreams of. Dreams he likewise gave to me, as I drifted into sleep to his words from Stephanie's mouth, floating like a ball punted by the goalie back into play.

(March 6)

45. Gucci

I WAS WALKING through campus today at class change time, which, when it's really hopping, reminds me of hustling (or moseying) between classes in our very big high school with the very narrow hallways, one of which, A-Hall it was called, was a mile long. It was a little bit like cattle through chutes. High school in general, maybe school in general, at its common worst anyway, is a little bit like cattle through chutes. And as I was walking, dodging the children whose heads are in their phones and the children on the new motorized skateboards that look fun as hell, I was noticing, as I often do, how difficult it can be sometimes for boys to smile. It sometimes feels as though there's a prohibition on boys smiling, chronic among these Midwestern boys, but I've seen it flare up elsewhere, and it reminds me that when

I was about twelve years old I'd wake up sometimes furrowing my brow. Practicing, I guess, at being a boy? Anyway, the prohibition on smiling (which, I know, might be the inverse of the prohibition on girls *not* smiling), I mean the prohibition on *noncompulsory* smiling, even if it's only temporary, or regional, or occasional, constitutes one of the grave destitutions, the grave sorrows, of being a boy, or a man, or a male, or whatever you call that creature whose life span is shorter in no small part because he's not supposed to smile.

But not this kid, this kid's got a long life in front of him, I thought, noticing him smiling his pretty smile very big—extra pretty now that the mask mandate has just been lifted; more face, etc.—at the young woman he was walking with, to whom I overheard him ask, smilingly, *Do you know what Gucci means?* And the way he asked it, with such genuine and tender curiousity, made me certain that either this person was seventy years old, in which case I have to ask her what kind of lotion she uses, or she was from another country. Maybe Nebraska. For those of you over seventy or from another country, thinking Gucci is a fashion line, alligator bags and cologne favored by Slick Rick, you're right, but that wasn't the smiling kid's question. The smiling kid's question was what Gucci *means*, which these days you can look up in Merriam- (wait, who's Merriam?)

Webster's Words at Play section for the most monotone vanilla ironyless definition on earth: "fancy, very fashionable; great, excellent."

And though the word *Gucci* to mean "deluxe" is a delight, as are the inventions (and interventions!) we make of words, and the overheard flirtations, and the sun making at last a crack in the gray sky, none are as delightful as this kid smiling, or, better yet, the two of them smiling at each other. And how I could see so.

(March 9)

46. Helmets Free

TODAY, AFTER SHOOTING some hoops with Jared up in Easton, then spinning around the neighborhood looking for old buildings we might convert into dreamy basketball courts, we got a couple smoothies at the Public Market, and past us whooshes a parade of kids doing wheelies on Northampton Street, swerving sometimes between cars to keep the wheelies going. *Wheelie gangs*, Jared called them, pointing and smiling, before asking if we have those in Bloomington, which we do not, at least not in my neighborhood, which seems to have few children, and where there are children, if they are out of your sight and not at a lesson or practice or some kind of improvement session, they wear two or three helmets. And probably elbow pads to boot. The children in my neighborhood, so many of the children these days, seem to wear wrist guards and tracking devices and take a water bottle and their cellphones to get the mail. My god, it filled me up, this parade of helmet-less children veering their precious little lawless brains through traffic on one wheel with nary a parent to be seen. Now *that* gave me hope.

(March 19)

47. The Complimentary Function

I'M SPENDING A few days in Columbus on my way back from my nana's memorial in Youngstown—convalescing, it feels like; I'm pooped from all this mourning—and I found myself a good healthy joint to eat lunch at. A not quite but almost disheveled place that had the feeling of someone's house, which, for the record, I love. Less likely to get in trouble, maybe. There were a couple bookshelves with quite used books. There was stuff you couldn't tell whether or not it was for sale. Cups and linens maybe. Wool socks maybe. They definitely had some local produce and a bunch of vegan cheesecake. Though I didn't find any, I wouldn't have been too surprised to have found some magazines on the back of the toilet, some shaving cream on the sink.

As I was poring over their abundant menu, a young white-looking server who had the kind of authority and moxie that made me think she probably owned the place, which maybe included wearing a tube top on a day it was flurrying outside, came over to my table and said, "I like your style." I looked at her, not sure I heard her right, and asked, "Excuse me?" She said, "You have great style," drawing one quick brushstroke through the air with her free hand as though to further articulate her point: "all this." For the record I was wearing a shimmery lavender button-up shirt I snagged at the thrift store in Hellertown for my nana's memorial beneath an old-ish winter vest, jeans rolled up into floods (my pants often end up being floods, so I roll them up, pre-emptively flooding them before some mean middle-schooler notices them and starts teasing me about them), and light green sneakers. Though I agreed with her, it was a little bit challenging for me to believe she agreed with her, which skepticism was confirmed, sort of maybe, when I noticed her complimenting every single person who came through those doors, or who she was ringing up. *Oh, I love your shoes*, and *oh, your hair is great*, and *oh*—waving her hand through the air at someone dressed very unlike me; better, we might both agree—*I love your style.*

Although who doesn't want their style to be singularly complimented by their server with great style, I don't think I felt bereft or robbed or, necessarily, anything that would imply scarcity in the complimentable world. More, I was reminded this is a recent common experience, always (as I recall) at a food or beverage establishment, mostly administered by white or white-looking women, such that today I thought, watching this person machine-gun compliments to someone they were serving, *Oh, they teach that at white girl school.* Where they also teach the word *perfect* to mean "fine," or "okay," which strikes me as a kind of apocalyptic optimism. Also at that school, they teach that paradoxical, stammery grammatical construction, *yeah no.*

I wonder if the complimentary function came into the common-ish white-girl repertoire by virtue of some movie or show or TikTok or something, a phenomenon I have witnessed, always retrospectively, people suddenly doing the exact same thing, a phrase or hand movement or facial gesture, and I learn, now I'm talking about boys, who have their own schools, *oh, they were all doing Jim Carrey*, or *oh, they were all being characters in a Bud or Miller Light commercial*, which, because such affects are contagious, so was I.

Damn, I'm a character in a Jim Carrey movie I've never even seen and probably, if it's not *Eternal Sunshine of the Spotless Mind*, I would think it's goofy. I'm a goofy character in a goofy movie. Or, and this is even worse, *Damn, I'm a character in a beer commercial.* Or worse still: *Damn, I'm a character in a faculty meeting*, I recently shuddered, hearing myself use the new ubiquitous professorial faux-inquiristic prefatory stammer, *right?*, which in that ballpark sidles up next to the word *problematic*, another academical word I kind of hate and sometimes catch myself saying when what I really mean is *fucked up*.

No one can dispute it's nice being complimented—just as it's nice complimenting—but it makes me wonder about the utility of the gesture, and I'm not actually talking about tips, I'm talking about survival. Which, you're right, tips is. I'm talking about the studied complimentary function as analogous or the same as what the massage therapist noted upon meeting me, doing her intake (which, in addition to height and weight and previous surgeries also involved, pretty sure, looking at my field) said to me, unsmilingly, almost with pity, "You're always smiling, aren't you? Always have that big smile. Wonder what's behind that."

(March 26)

48 Early!

TODAY I WAS (weirdly) early for a meeting on the porch of the coffee shop, and after I confirmed I had not mixed up the dates and was in the right place (not a sure bet with me), instead of preparing a little more for the meeting which probably I could've stood doing, I exhaled hard, took a slow and ponderous sip of my coffee, and looked around: at the scamper of birds into the crabapple tree; the sunflowers and forsythia growing across the way; someone going by with a boom box in the basket of his bike blasting Bobby Brown; two people saying goodbye in such a way that I suspected they were falling in love; and eventually, reluctantly, dutifully, my cellular telephone, which said, *So sorry I'm late*, and which I made reply, *No sweat take your time*, though what I really meant was *No sweat take your sweet time. Bump into a friend. Take a call. Get down on your hands and knees and dip your face like a ladle into the hyacinths. I'm grateful you're late.* Which I guess you might attribute to feeling, like I bet a lot of the kids these days do, overscheduled. Too many meetings. But it might also be that earliness, maybe especially earliness on account of someone or something else's lateness, can feel like the universe just dropped a bouquet of time, and often a luminous bouquet of time, in your lap. (Also worth noting: a few years back when I had a doctor's appointment, the doctor was very late, by which I became very early, though because the equivalent of Jerry Springer was screaming on the television beneath the subtly bludgeonous fluorescent lighting doing its job of making us look even sicker than we were, I walked my early ass out of there. Nothing's always anything, I guess I'm trying to say.)

Perhaps no place is better at producing one's earliness than the airport, given as planes are not infrequently late, and given as, not always but often, I'm rushing to catch them. In this case, time, which is scant and sinister as I'm driving too fast to the airport, becomes, when I jog to the check-in machine praying security's not a mess and see on the board that my flight is delayed two hours, spacious as the sky in Montana. Even if on the other side of that flight is someone or something I really want to see or do, a late plane usually tickles me. If I was the kind of person to say *oh goody*, I would say *oh goody*, as I exhale, amble through security extra chipper suddenly, and then mosey about the airport like it's a mall, which airports these days kind of are. I look to see if there are any books worth reading (some airports have good bookstores these days). I flip through a magazine or two. I hit all the water fountains. I even inspect the vending machines, which vend so many things these days. I avert my eyes from any television flickering news hell. If I'm early enough, I might cruise over to another terminal, maybe all the terminals depending, to see how they do it in the hinterlands (usually the same). I might find an empty spot and do some pushups or lunges. But the most enticing part of the airport—which is already sparklingly liminal, and sparkles more when you are newly early, earlier still as your flight gets delayed some more—is the people, who are always very interesting, but a little extra interesting in airports.

The last time I was early for a flight on account of the flight being delayed, at La Guardia, a little boy and his father sat down next to me, and I could gather, with my limited Spanish, that the child was to deliver this small fold of cash to his mother and no one else, which the father was tucking into the boy's interior jacket pocket as the boy played a video game on a tablet. The boy said, *Okay*, then as he was zooming the car through a course, periodically crashing and burning, he started singing to himself, which struck me that day as the most beautiful, luckiest thing in the world. And further down the terminal on one of my laps I watched two people, mother and daughter they looked like, holding hands and looking out the window at the plane departing for Chicago, the daughter trying hard not to cry, and failing when her mom pulled her close. A little further I spied a woman the spitting image of my nana tucking some cash into her bra, which, too, my nana did. And as I went to get some water, a woman was standing with her hand on the fountain, not drinking, and when I noticed she was obviously studying the birds darting above and said to her, *Yeah, aren't they great*, she glanced and smiled at me quickly before looking back up, whispering, *I'm trying to get them some water*, which I'm guessing the birds had covered, along with the food, but c'mon now Ross, that's beside the point.

(March 28)

49. Be Direct

I LEFT WALLY'S café today a little bit earlier than I intended because I needed to use the loo, but someone got in there and stayed in there, for ten, maybe fifteen minutes, which signaled to me *poor thing their tummy*, though that didn't console what was happening in my tummy, so I got, and quickly too, booking on my bike to the nearest academic building, where I speed-walked to a loo, burst through the bathroom door, then the stall door, then hustled my belt free and pants down and thank god sat down in time, just. (NB: *In time* means, as in this case, "with time to spare"; "on or with the beat"; or "inside of, or congruent with, time itself." Just noting it.) Sitting there I started reading what is posted on the inside of every (male or gender-neutral) bathroom door on my campus, which are tips or strategies for avoiding and interrupting sexual assault, which is a lot of *Keep an eye on your drunk friends, all of them.*

Because I use the loo where I work not infrequently, and because I am my most readerly on a toilet emptying myself (reading a kind of refill?), whether it's graffiti or Tolstoy or a list of suggestions on how we might hurt each other less, I read this set of instructions a lot. Though for some reason today I read them a little closer, particularly the imperative to BE DIRECT, by which we are instructed to go directly to the person, or persons, who appear to be in danger, and to ask plainly: *Are you okay?*

I was reminded of the time a few years ago that I was walking up to a new restaurant in town and as I approached I saw some people on the ground, which, from afar looked maybe like people playing, tickling, or wrestling; but as I got closer, I realized it was a woman who had pinned a boy face down under her leg, her son I presume, who was trying to army crawl free to no avail because she was also holding him with her left hand, and with her right hand she was smacking the hell out of his ass. I mean goddamn, she was wearing his ass out.

I don't know the calculations that went through my head as I was approaching, though I assure you it was more than any supercomputer on this planet, any self-driving algorithmic doohickey they got out there, I promise. Among the many variables—not close to all of them, by the way—were that the child being struck seemed to be a boy, the blows were contained in the ass region (not the head), and he was probably about ten or eleven (not three or four). Also, I guess, this: I am the child of a mother who sometimes wanted to wear my ass out, and if her hands didn't bruise so easily, she might've. Ask her. Anyhow, my brains were whirling as I approached them, the mother's bare arms flexed, corralling and whacking this boy, who was trying like hell to scuttle away, and without really deciding to, probably because I didn't know what else to do, I asked the mother, softly as I knew how, *Are you okay?* Which, in retrospect, was probably a gentle way to hopefully slow something down, or bring it to a halt. *Hopefully,* which is why I was scared when I heard it come out of my mouth, because within the realm of possibility was my *are you okay* enflaming this woman to lean more into the ass whooping, or worse, start beating my ass! (Just kidding, my ass could've taken it. Nor could she have caught me to beat it. But still, and seriously, I was nervous.)

It was a little bit like the plug being pulled out, or how Nipsey Russell in *The Wiz* just stops moving when his oil runs dry—a few gradually softening blows, her release of the boy, who got to his feet and ran away, and the tears, which came out suddenly, and hard, replacing the blows it seemed, as she looked at me, or sort of looked through me, shaking her head and saying, very quietly, *no.*

(April 1)

50. Imposter (Syndrome)

I WAS TALKING with a friend today who, like me, teaches college, and who, like me, isn't white, and so ends up advising, as we do, because of the dearth of us as much as how awesome we are, many of the black and nonwhite students in our programs. Eventually we got talking about that condition familiar to all our advisees, and ourselves, familiar indeed to almost everyone in the realm of academia or the academia-adjacent-world: Imposter Syndrome. It is a condition much fretted about. There are workshops and symposia, I assure you. There are paid consultants to help you with it. Soon there will be a certificate, if not a degree, in its alleviation, I assure you.

The syndrome, with which I, too, have been afflicted, I mean *afflicted*—one time calling my friend

Joanna because I was so convinced I had no idea how to teach a class on *Uncle Tom's Cabin* (which I put on the goddamn syllabus!) that I needed her to talk me through, or off, the ledge; one time introducing a fellow nonwhite writer to my mostly white department like I was suddenly possessed by the wind or something, my voice *quaking*, I mean quaking; a few (hundred) other times—emerges, so the workshops will tell you (I'm saving you money and time!), from a feeling of inadequacy often experienced by certain people, often nonwhite people, first-generation or working-class types (these categories often overlap, as you know). They (we) feel like they (we) don't belong, because they (we) don't, and so to prove they (we) do, they (we) are often the ones jotting most quickly at the meetings, writing words like *heuristic* and *impanel*, and they (we) are very careful not to break anything, and whose hands, if they (we) are not actively eating with the so many spoons and forks at the faculty dinner, are in their (our) laps.

The people not so afflicted, you can see them a mile away, and if they do not come from money, which they mostly do, they come from PhDs (or PhD-adjacents), my anecdotal research tells me. (It's also possible a very few of them dip their bucket into a well of okay-ness I have not yet located.) They really stretch out like they own the place, because they know they kind of do. About these people by these people such things are said as *he just looks like he should be a full professor*, regardless that he hasn't written a book in a decade or two, much the way some people think Gavin Newsom just looks like a president.

Anyhow, as we were talking, it occurred to me that the syndrome is a symptom of wanting to be taken seriously by the people who run the joint, or, another way of putting it: of *wanting to belong.* Who wants to be an interloper? Or a better way of saying it still, who wants to be *perceived* as an interloper? As we unlock the door to our offices, or as we walk to the front of our classes, or as we introduce this or that fancy speaker, or introduce ourselves to this or that fancy person, we do not want someone to wonder, or god forbid actually ask, *What are they* (we) *doing here?*

It's worth noting that niggling inside this Imposterism is the knowledge that some people say things about black, etc., college teachers like, *oh they were an affirmative action hire*, etc. It's a way of saying, *we all know you weren't hired because of the quality of your work*, and by extension, *you were only hired because you're black, etc.*, and by extension, *you don't belong here.* The implication is that *they*, however, were hired for the quality of their work—*as used to happen in the good old days, when merit existed*—and not because they went to the same schools and knew the same people and had the same advisors and talked just like and ate the same foods as and summered in the same places as the people hiring them. In other words, as though they weren't affirmative action hires. Look, I'm all ears if you think you have a good argument for merit, but this sure as hell ain't one.

In other words, and here's where I'm gonna earn my money (this is also the [long-coming, my bad!] delight): for those of you (us) suffering from Imposterism, what happens when, aside from keeping our jobs and insurance, we reflect a little on the institution we are pining to be accepted by—of which pining, remember, the Imposterism is evidence—and realize that while we may enjoy teaching and writing and the big inexpensive gym and the libraries and all the serviceberry bushes on campus and the light on the limestone walls in the late afternoon and all the pudgy squirrels and the undergrads studiously feeding those squirrels from their own lunches—that maybe most of all—we may not, some of us anyway, be that interested in *belonging to the institution.* We may love school, for instance, as I now do—Ms. Cameron, my wonderful eleventh-grade English teacher, in whose class I was a bonafide jagoff numbskull, will be startled and, I bet, glad to hear—and we may love that it pays the bills, but we may not be that into the corporation it has become. Like, really. Not to mention those jackets with the decorative elbow patches. A sartorial effect matched in dismalness only by the truly petite pockets of some women's clothing. Maybe a few other things, fine.

Which unbelonging requires some discipline, some practice, because, and this is purely conjectural, speculative, I think Imposterism is often co-diagnosed with optimistic-diversity-thought, the belief (hope!) that if we apply a little elbow grease and keep a good attitude our very presence in the institution will transform that institution. *Changing it from the inside*, we sing-say, throwing cute little uppercuts through the air. And as tribute to such belief, we have pinned to the bulletin boards in our imaginations the photograph of the little black child touching the first black president's hair, identifying—and plucking our heartstrings as he does so—the texture of the president's hair as like his, and therefore, we all get it, he, too, might be president. And because heartstrings are often used as garrotes, we forget that the door that's been kicked open for that child and other children "like" him, or ceiling smashed or summit climbed or whatever, is to a job whose description, in addition to the ceremonial stuff and pictures, is to disproportionately withhold the means of life—whether by letting the water stay poisoned, drone-bombing civilians, couping and starving (my bad; *sanctioning*) uncooperative regimes, etc.—from people the complexion, ballpark, of that child. In other words, sometimes belonging means we, too, now might push the terrible buttons.

If that's the summit, Lord that we might all be imposters.

(April 2)

51. The Tagolog Word for Which

TODAY I WAS a guest in a class my friend was teaching about wonder, and in what was very much not a wonder, I almost inadvertently blew it off, and would've, had I not by some stroke of luck peeked at my calendar. This happens to me not infrequently, a deadline or time-sensitive obligation that I've spaced out on smacks me in the face, then I shout and freak out for a second before, in this case, slapping on some clothes, stuffing my backpack, and jumping on my bike to campus, all the while thinking, swear to god, *This is good pedagogy, they might one day forgive themselves for their own lateness*, which I actually stand by.

Anyhow, I was a guest not because they had read any of my books, at least a couple of which maybe could've fit the curriculum, but because they had read my friend and sometimes collaborator Aimee Nezhukumatathil's book, *World of Wonders*. Turns out they had perused, -ish, maybe two or three of my delights as a kind of supplement, I guess, to Aimee's book, which, oh no, what if my tardiness was in fact passive aggression about being Robin to Aimee's Batman, say it ain't so!!! I think it probably ain't so. I'm late when they've read my book, too.

We had a good conversation about Aimee's book, after which I dropped into a local coffee shop near campus that I infrequently frequent, where I bought an espresso (doppio, sans saucer), ducked into the back room where the low ceilings and shitty tile and grimy light and extra seating are, and I saw my friend Nandi, visiting from Detroit, posted up at my favorite corner table, the one with all the lyric graffiti. I must've looked like I was having a stroke, or maybe a revelation, for I was stricken, mid-stride, mouth open, eyes big, until she saw me, got up, and oh we hugged two and a half years' worth of hug, we groaned, we giggled, we put each other at risk of bodily harm, for which, in the Filipino language of Tagolog—Patrick Rosal writes about it in his poem "Delenda Undone"—there is a word. I almost never go to this coffee shop anymore; I almost went to the one in the hotel. Yadda yadda grace. Yadda yadda *delight*.

We visited, laughed very loud like we do, turning heads with our laughter as we do, a few tears forming in the corners of Nandi's eyes as we did so. We kept kicking each other under the table, sometimes for emphasis I think, sometimes, at least for me, it's strange to say so but I think it's true, to confirm that she was really here. My foot saying, again and again, *It's you*. I also noticed, as we talked in this grimy back room where after the toilet's flushed you can hear it rush by in the exposed PVC pipe just above your head, that Nandi really listens in conversation, which, coupled with her caring about me maybe, and a few other things, is maybe why she also sometimes disagrees with me. As we were talking, and I was remembering her face, her voice, her laugh, how she moves her hands or how she thinks, I thought, very clearly, *this person is beloved to me*.

We made plans to catch up in a day or two, share some poems, maybe get some food, etc. And then we hugged again the Tagolog word for which, I got back on my bike, more leisurely this time, and I'm not saying it was embracing my beloved friend after a long time, nor am I saying it wasn't, but one way or the other I noticed, pedaling home, that the serviceberry bushes had all bloomed.

(April 11)

52. Truly Overnight Sometimes It Seems

IT IS TRULY overnight sometimes it seems that the dandelions put on their crowns, and just like that, the world is suddenly brighter, more abundant, more possible—this, of course, if you, like me, adore the dandelion, see their unmartial ranks suddenly outflanking the gloom, outflowering the doom, and if you, like me, make love (a little much?) with its absolutely usable body, body of utter benevolence, body of total beneficence, petite and profligate and gleeful lovenote: the roots for all kinds of medicine, not to mention your various probiotic, bitter, hot morning drinks (for the caffeine-weaning among us); the flowers, which are actually (get close—no, *closer*—you'll see what I mean) a million flowers, which the pollinators bloom into a winged dancefloor at our feet; and the leaves, little lion's teeth, which, in addition to throwing them into your tomato sauce or greens or smoothie or black-eyed-pea fritters, you might do like this:

handful or two of leaves, chopped
flour of your choice (cornmeal, chickpea, lentil,
whole wheat)
onion
garlic powder
paprika
salt
baking powder
water enough to get it all to a clumpy, dandy
consistency

Fry in oil on low heat. Or bake them.

You can use the flowers for this, too, which can probably be a way of managing or curtailing their reproduction—they fuck like bunnies: those million flowers turn into a million seeds turn into a million million dandelions turn to a million million seeds, all of which is to say, the dandelion giggles at the capitalistic (and monotheistic [No other god but me & etc.] and pop song monogamistic [no one will ever love you like I do & etc.]) myth of scarcity for which it must be destroyed, and quick!—which I have no interest in doing, for they are my most consistent, prolific, generous, trouble- and labor-free crop. I mean, when the squash bugs get the squash, and the cabbage moths the collards, and the blight the tomatoes, the dandelions are steady Freddy. They are the Draymond Greens and Marcus Smarts of the garden. The Brian Grants. The Mo Cheekses or Bobby Joneses. The Patrick Beverleys. They always show up and give their all. We need to give them their flowers!

They are also little beacons of the *it'll be okay*, and if they had a soundtrack, it would be "O-o-h Child." Maybe their prettiness, by which I really mean *beauty*, is because their roots go so far down, they fathom the depths (which, pretty sure, also explains their nutritive profile: Kale can't hold dandelion's jockstrap), and those beautiful flowers are missives from the deep. Or the dark. Or the mystery. Or the unknown. Or the underworld. Whichever word we want to use today to mean the dead, or at least the dead-adjacent. Missives from the dead, these little festive blooms. To which, I don't know about you, but I'm trying to listen.

(April 15)

53. Not This Dog

TODAY WE ARE babysitting Georgia's two dogs, Niko, and Millie. Niko is a stately, protective, self-possessed if mournful brindle bantamweight, and Millie is an anxious, rambunctious, pawing little muscleball whose imagination seems always to be ablaze. At this moment they are curled together at the foot of the bed, down near my feet, and Tucker, their older brother, or maybe he's their uncle, a much smaller guy but still their boss somehow, is at the other side of the bed, crying a little bit about whatever he's dreaming. I hope those are cries of delight. I hope he's dreaming of dunking a basketball.

Twenty minutes ago, when I was making my second cup of coffee, all three of them, like a team, walked one after the other to the one water bowl and lapped—each one with a slightly different cadence and volume to their lap. As Niko, a truly distinguished and debonair creature if ever there was one, walked past me after drinking behind his two buddies, strutting almost at having commingled so nonchalant, it occurred to me that it seemed not even to cross his mind, sophisticate though he is, to ask for his own water bowl.

It got me thinking about Niko's tolerance for putting his nose and tongue to things I might prefer not to, and how all of the dogs have been known to chew up dead and disgusting things, and that Millie time to time gobbles (and defecates) dirty socks out of the laundry, which mostly do not come out on their own, by which I mean her mother, Georgia, has had to extract these dirty socks now somewhat dirtier having been passed through her (the dog's) intestinal tract, gagging (the mother) the whole time. I'm not saying they don't have their issues (one might say eating socks is an issue), but what is not their issue, and for this I think on their behalf *how lucky*, I think *Oh this is what they mean by prelapsarian*, is filth, or being filthy, or, and maybe this is the real rub, being perceived as such. In fact, they seem not to even know what filth means, and are a little bit like gross little grubby human children this way, who are also, so often—I know it's a cliché to say so but it's true—our teachers.

(April 16)

54. I'd Prefer Not To

I WAS WALKING into town today, and I ran into a lovely guy I used to see all the time—in the Afghan joint, acupuncture joint, walking the streets, etc.—though it's been a while. You know how it is. He was walking his charmingly aloof dog, a petite squirt who was sniffing around in one of the prettiest gardens in town, while inside the house about ten feet away were a couple dogs crashing against the windows and walls to get out here so they could murder this little aloof fella, who was peeing on their peonies.

When I asked how it's been going—implying *how's it been going these last couple years*, the shitshow—he shrugged, and he smiled sort of puzzledly, because his business, which is called PR, did not take a hit like many other businesses did. In fact, in the midst of the crisis, it kind of took off, he said, in that sort of I'm-happy-but-I-know-I-shouldn't-be way that is so common these days. He explained to me that PR is no longer only for humans, but also for a bunch of acronyms I did not understand though I knew enough to know to get nervous knowing the acronyms exist. The one I remembered was NFT, which, when he said it, I interrupted him to ask what that stands for. *Nonfungible token.* Whatever that is, it evidently needs a PR campaign.

Then we got around to Megan Thee Stallion, who, if I understood it right, and it's very likely I didn't, because I was nervous, panicking a little, though trying to keep up, is doing a tour where I think the audience—I suspect this means thousands and thousands of people; I'm guessing Megan Thee Stallion isn't playing small venues these days—will all put on virtual reality—I'm sorry, I mean VR—helmets, umm, I guess, together. I guess that's what some people these days are calling together. Apart together. Together apart. However they say it. Anyway, they're doing PR for that VR show, too, which I think meant, maybe this was the flicker in his eyes, the gleam, that PR no longer needs there to be a "there there." At which point you can start printing your own moola. I know nothing about the financial system, but I have seen *The Big Short* about six times, and I'm pretty sure the great innovation in there—maybe it was derivatives; maybe it was bundled mortgages; maybe it was CDOs; maybe I better go watch *The Big Short* a seventh time—was inventing out of thin air a mechanism, a great golden way, to make a small handful of people rich. Sidenote but no biggie also making many large many many handfuls of people homeless. For or by what we might in another frame of mind call a conspiracy theory. I.e., a no there there.

Anyway, I was trying to be a sport and track what was being said to me despite feeling like the great, whirling, ravenous void from *Evil Dead II* was opening up in my chest and sucking me and everything I could perceive or imagine into it, and I heroically managed to cling to the true living world in part by noticing the espaliered apple tree against the picket fence behind this very sweet PR man, and that what had been just a few days prior the still tightly wrapped buds kissed with pink (I pass this tree daily) were now open. As his lips continued moving, I watched, just behind him, little pollinators swirling around and into the new blooms. I nodded and smiled and *mmhhhmmed* until he said, *Well, I better get back to work. Take care now*, waving sweetly over his shoulder as he and his dog trotted away.

You do the same, I said, moving to the tree, which now seemed almost to be opening its arms to me. I put my face to a few of the flowers and inhaled. And I brushed my lips against them while doing so. A honeybee was scooting through the neighbor bloom. I took one more deep breath and headed up the street. And there goes the magnolia tree. And there goes the cardinal. And there goes that woman with the bad limp and the big smile. And there goes that sweet Tacoma with the long bed good for hauling. And there goes Jim, who just retired from the community radio station, looking at his garden, smiling. And there goes the lilac and there goes the bunny, and there goes the brick walkway and the breeze and the bird shit splatting from the mulberry tree. And there goes that hiccup in my heart. And there goes my favorite alley. And there goes the rust in my knee. And there goes that pink dogwood tree. And there goes the sound of two people fighting behind me. Oh wait. They're laughing. They're laughing and touching each other. Arm in arm they are, I see now, it's glee.

(April 18)

55. Improvised Pocket Parks

I WAS WALKING to the store to get some groceries, looking for a warm nook to sit in, a place I might scoop up some sun, wake up my sleepy melanin, which is not the easiest thing to do in this town. I don't mean unhibernating my melanin, I mean finding the public place in which to do so, which in plenty of other places are in abundance. But in these parts, it's slim pickings. "These parts" is a geographical project above my pay grade (I loathelove that stupid, meaningfully meaningless phrase), but I do wonder about how regions, and the people who people them, do (or not) common places. One meager, possibly dingbat, and kind of counterintuitive theory is that if a region is less populated there will be less public space, and perhaps more private. Another has to do with money—counterintuitive again, but so proven as to be obvious: the more money, the more richness, the less public space, i.e., the more likely you are to be trespassing. Another has to do with when and from where the most recent settlers arrived. Another, ancillary to the previous, is how mixed—religion, ethnicity, etc.—the area is. Climate matters, too, I bet. Obviously, this is another book—*The Book of Public Space*—and it ought to have beautiful colorful and somewhat lyrical graphs like the ones in *W. E. B. Du Bois's Data Portraits: Visualizing Black America.*

Long story short: there's no pocket parks here, so I find myself looking for seams in the propertized world—so often, know it or not, we are looking for seams in the propertized world—ideally south-facing, to sit down and stretch out, listen to birds, write a few sentences. Rub that sun all over my body, as Richard Pryor as Mudbone I think put it. The seams take different forms for me: an alley, a milk crate behind a convenience store, a low wall in the cemetery. But today it's a church. In fact, it's a church I have frequented, not for the eucharist inside, but for the one that comes in June from the two cherry trees, one tart and one sweet, out front. My friend Chris showed them to me. Baptized me I guess, for they were the first cherry trees I'd ever harvested from. I was inside this church once, too, invited to a day of shape note singing, which I cannot really explain aside from saying it is old-timey, gothic, and punk-rock Holy Roller-y all at once, and if there was a little less burning in hell, which took a sec to detect given how otherworldly the choiring, Stephanie and I might've stayed longer than ten minutes.

On the side of that church is a staircase going to a double door. And though staircases make excellent pocket parks, it is also the case that they often lead to someone's home or business—someone's property. Which is to say, they are excellent though *temporary* pocket parks. But a church is different. Or it ought to be anyway. A church, belonging to God, who is everywhere and everything, kind of belongs to everyone. Seems to me, anyway. And if you get kicked off the steps of a church, well goddamn—we better turn that church into a library or basketball court or something.

Anyhow, this is a good godly spot: full sun, comfortable stairs, and across the alley is a lilac bush blooming against a house the color blue that makes me want to congratulate and thank whoever lives there. From this tucked-away staircase you can see the passersby, and the passersby can see you, if they look, which, being in a pocket, they mostly don't. But one person did, and she smiled a little bit and waved.

(May 2)

56. The Purple Iris Angel

TODAY, IN A Zoom meeting, having not yet hidden my self-view, I noticed my neck, as I age, and get a bit thinner, and was reminded, again, that I favor my father as he looked at the end of his life, which happened, in an official or conventional sense, exactly eighteen years ago today. His death is about a senior in high school today. His death today is old enough to vote or join the service and go die for the interests of wealthy people. But not quite old enough to get a drink. That'll be in three years, and how sweet it would have been to share a drink with my father after his death, by which I mean how badly sometimes I wish to talk with him after the understanding—whatever it might be—afforded him by his death, which, weird to say but I think it's true, belongs to me as much as it does him. Me and other people I mean, but I'm the one writing the essay.

I do my best to acknowledge this day, which usually means talking to my mother on the phone, but might also mean putting on his slippers, or at least noticing they're there. Which, a few times, I have forgotten to do. Neglected is what it feels like, wrong is what I mean, until I get into his slippers and think maybe also cause for something like celebration, something like—this from in my father's slippers—*I appreciate your concern, I truly do, but please remember my death was not the most important part of my life. Or, I hope, yours.*

For example, the deep blue irises with gold speckling inside you are walking by at this very moment.

For example, how everything some days looks like angels.

(May 10)

57. Tag and Such

I WAS WALKING between the neighborhoods today and saw, much to my delight, a group of kids playing tag. And compounding the delight, I saw no adults nearby. If there was any supervision, it was by the older kids who I could tell very quickly were good at the game—they had "no tag backs" down pat. *The simple game*, I thought. No, it was: *Ahhhh, the simple game*, more like that. The tinkling bells or chimes of revery, a few unostentatious beams of light suddenly piercing the clouds to let you know I am now in my mind both delighted at and cataloging the simple games, the unalienated, un-virtual games, the games of arms and legs and feet and hands and every once in a while blood and tears and such, of which tag is one of the apotheoses. *One of*. Others include all manner of human-body races:

running, up a tree, from seated to standing, down a flight of stairs, etc. Duck, Duck, Goose is a variety of the race, with a touch of touching tossed in. And then there's tug-of-war of course, simple, brute, the strategizing—*Pull! Pull!*—dumb. Four square's another, a game to which I have forgotten the rules but know that I would quickly dominate on the elementary school courts, though its single-celled ancestor, I'm pretty sure, is catch. Just as dodgeball's single-celled ancestors are throwing and ducking. Wrestling. Fights. Mercy. Spitting for distance. Plucking knuckles. Loudest yell/clap/burp/fart, etc. Skipping stones, though elegant and lyrical, and though it can turn into a game of searching and collecting—and contemplating, as you're doing so, the river of life and eternity, etc.—is really just throwing rocks on the water.

Almost always the simple games expand, or evolve, or blend, into slightly more complex versions. For instance, in our neighborhood we played a game called manhunt, elsewhere called ghosts in the graveyard, probably elsewhere called personhunt, which is actually hide and seek *plus* tag at night with a larger field of play in which, instead of just finding or just tagging, you track down and apprehend. (Less cooties, more incarceration.) Because we lived in a big apartment complex, our games of manhunt could easily have ten or twelve kids to a team. If anything got complicated about manhunt—aside from the emotional complications of hiding so well no one finds you, or hiding so well you start hearing creepy stuff and get scared, or hiding close to your friend who you silently watch get wrangled and dragged away—it was the concept of *jail*, which in our neighborhood was usually some stairs, or maybe a light pole, where the captured would have to hang around, attended to by a guard who defended, or tried to defend, the jail from being *sprung*, which was really hard to do, and it's from what the liberators screamed upon unshackling their teammates that manhunt gets one of its less carceral and more optimistic and emancipatory names: *Spring.*

(May 11)

58. Paper Menus (and Cash!)

DAVE AND I got together for breakfast today at the Owlery, the vegetarian place in town with owls for a theme. I don't know about you, but when restaurants, or people, have themes, I'm always like, *What's up with the owls?* I don't mean disparagingly or dismissively what's up with the owls. I mean with curiosity. I mean was it a book? Was it a dream? Was it a dead favorite uncle who loved, or looked like, or was, an owl? Or maybe it's more like style, the trappings of style, something you try out, or do, until it starts to do you, and if you're James Harden, whose nickname is now *The Beard*, you're sometimes like, *damn I wish I could shave this beard*. Or if you're my friend Rachel, who only wears orange Converse, your heart breaks a little bit at the beautiful purple pair on the rack you know you won't be getting. Or if you're the owls restaurant and someone brings you a beautiful velvet bald eagle teddy bird you say *oh, thank you,* then tearfully toss it in the trash out back. Or if you're me, and you like to wear rubber bands—yes, *wear,* it's fashion, inherited from my father, there's a story (or two)—enough that you walk the earth half-scanning for rubber bands, periodically endowing them with a magical, salvational quality—i.e., this is the rubber band that will keep the airplane in the sky; i.e., that is the rubber band (middle of a busy street) that is going to keep the baby safe. Which is to say, style can tip into pathology. So heads up for that.

The masked server asked us if we could use the QR code or if we would need a paper menu. I hate to tell you, by which I really mean it delights me to tell you, that though I submit to more nefarious shit every second of every day, I will not submit to that. And as much as the telling you is a delight, the not submitting, the refusal, is way more. The refusal is joy.[1] The refusal is among the offenses of joy. Though Dave was in the streets about the collaboration between the CIA and the Contras, which allowed cocaine to flood American cities in order to fund the antisocialist forces in the early

1 We sometimes forget that one of joy's primary expressions is refusal—I will not support your war; I will not accept your policy; I will not obey your law; I will not let you cut down this grove of trees—refusals that are the evidence (and practice) of belonging to something larger than yourself. Larger, too, and by far, than whom and what we refuse.

eighties, he also doesn't want to dwell on the miseries. Dave has kids who are the inheritors of this, I get it. It's one of the nice things about hanging out with him. Also, and maybe more to the point here, Dave's so old school he didn't really know what a QR code was, and so he was a little baffled at the exchange, which I explained to him by showing him the little evil square, telling him not to look directly into it, then pointing to his phone, then saying a bunch of stuff I guarantee you he stopped listening to before I got through it.

In the event that you haven't stopped listening, first: thank you, truly; and second: cash. Remember cash? Though there is no lament long or deep enough for the potential evils embedded in the abstraction of the earth and labor which maybe cash is, it's way cooler than the mandatory chip—i.e., digital modes of payment—which seems to me part of the general monitoring and surveillance regime we somehow almost overnight it seems got cool with. (Oh dear lord, someone just explained to me that it's now possible to use your palm to pay for stuff. Lest I go full-on apocalyptic, which I am wont sometimes to do, and which I have no doubt palm pay is evidence of [apocalypse; the bad kind], let me remind us of two of the zillion alternatives: 1. seeds; 2. the high five.) Not to mention, quiet as it's kept, not everyone has a bank account, or a card, and it seems to me those people ought to be able to get a coffee, too. I'm a dinosaur, I know.

The thing about paper menus is that they are most often kind of plastic, heartily laminated, but not this one. This one was printed on an elegant leaf of thick paper, and was quite unused, these days being these days. These days being these days, you can forget that part of the pleasure of the paper menu, laminated or not, is running your finger along its offerings, stopping at what sounds delicious, tapping it as a way of saying *ooh I might get this* to who you're with, who might do the same—which you might then do to the server, who might bend just slightly to consider what you're considering, to listen to you and help you. And when you're done ordering with a paper menu—and in this way it's like cash—you get to place it, with your actual precious hands if you have them, back into your server's actual precious hands. Which you might also do while making eye contact. And smiling. And saying thank you.

All of which we did![2] *(May 14)*

---

2 I know it might be tedious, and I know I might be close to undelightful ranting, but I'm going to take one more step toward us to suggest that any time we opt for the human interaction rather than the automated or digital one, which requires noticing how ubiquitous the automated or digital one has become (ubiquity makes invisibility, makes us look up from our machines and be like *where'd the people go?*)—checking out groceries; getting our ibuprofen; the menu thing; being in class; getting directions; finding or buying a book; learning how to do stuff—is a small act of revolt. Except there's no such thing as small revolt, because each revolt, even if only fleetingly, even if only for an instant, is making the world of our dreams.

59. Eat Candy! Destroy the State!

TODAY, AFTER I ordered my very small coffee—which the kind people at the café facilitated by allowing me to have a teeny cup with a refill for the price of the mug, which is for me among the delights (the small cup of coffee and the kind people who make it happen)—and was sipping and savoring it on the back steps, I wondered if the acute awareness of one's delights might likewise make one acutely aware of, or even acutely be the cause of, one's undelights. In other words, because I so love the small coffee, and now really know how much I love the small coffee, must I necessarily be disappointed or peeved when I am handed a disgusting huge twelve-ounce vat of coffee? Must it be like that time my mother, as usual, saving up her points on some stupid diet or other—isn't it strange, how many of us are constantly on some diet or other, battling, as we say, our weight, by which we mean our only bodies?—got up to Greenwood Dairies, the slightly scuzzy and totally delicious ice cream place up on Route 1 next to the pool hall and across from Denny's, and when she placed her order of vanilla peanut butter in a cup, and they told her they had just run out, she dropped her head into her hands and cried? Or if (when) someone puts mayonnaise on my veggie burger, or vegannaise, same gross diff, especially if I take a bite, and I think what's even the point of being alive anymore? Must it be like that? That, knowing how good good french fries are, bad ones must make you feel offended, aggressed, macroaggressed even? Must it?

No. It mustn't. And I will say it is a matter of maturity, or maybe more accurately or relevantly a matter of practice, that when they hand you the disappointing barrel of coffee, which in a certain (maybe underslept, dehydrated) mood can feel like a squelching, a murdering of delight, it's also the case that the barista was wearing a Milli Vanilli concert shirt. Not to mention that the song "Video Killed the Radio Star" that blasts your heart into a thousand butterflies every single time was playing on the algorithm machine. Or though the fries were ass, the ketchup was plenty. The vanilla peanut butter ice cream gone, but they had vanilla, not to mention those remarkably elegant wooden spoons, and, if you can get there through your tears, the trees from whom they come. For the record, I do not think of this as looking on the bright side, I think of it as looking at everything. Bad french fries do not negate good ketchup. That your one friend died does not untrue the fact that your other friend survived. Nor do such losses negate the huge crop of sweet potatoes from your garden, how your bike fits you, the quilt that came your way, the fact that dried beans are actually seeds that you can plant, and the delight of realizing that those two boys you thought were kneeling in prayer in the woods on campus were actually feeding the corpulent squirrels, which yeah, too, is a kind of prayer. And to suggest they ought to, diminishes everything.

Though my delight of record today—"the delight of record" is something I want to contest, for every delight is a delight of record, even if you don't record it with your pencil; it lodges in the body, particularly if you give it some lodging by noting it—is another little gnomic bit of truth, a mini haiku in all caps spray-painted on the rusty corrugated siding of a building that seems abandoned but who knows:

EAT CANDY!
DESTROY THE STATE!

(May 19)

60. At the End of a Photoshoot with My Friend Natasha, Walking Here and There Through the Orchard, Facing This Way, Then That, in Front of the Peach Tree

ME: “Wait, are you always walking around looking for the right light?”

NATASHA: “I guess you could say that.”

(May 20)

61. Friends Let Us Do Our Best Not to Leave This Life Having Not Loved What We Love Enough

I LEARNED TODAY from Dave that Joseph Fox Bookshop has gone out of business, I hope it wasn't "the pandemic," by which is really meant the lockdown policies that made the rich richer and kicked the shit out of most everyone else. (I just looked it up. It was.) Anyway, there is a cliché circulating these days like genital warts meant to suggest something was jarring or upsetting or super heart-stirring or something, I assure you someone is saying it at this very moment, I hate that I, too, am about to say it, but the news that Joseph Fox had closed felt like a gut punch. When Dave said it, I actually put my hand on my tummy and said *ughh*, and *no* and *why*, to which Dave shrugged and made a sad and sympathetic face. He loved the store, too.

Joseph Fox was a beautifully curated bookstore (for my tastes, which needn't be yours): lots of essays and nonfiction; lots of poems and novels; and nearly whole runs of certain presses' stuff (I think a bunch of the New York Review Books; that whole Melville House Last Interview series I think I remember; probably some of those petite Penguin Classics; and a bunch of the stout Archipelago bricks, books with which to make a house that won't blow down). They had a gardening section where I once got a seed-saving book, and an art section where I got a book of Anni Albers's work. It was small, the back room was very close to the front room, and the hallway between them was often packed, encouraging lots of *'scuse me*s and *after you*s and such, which are themselves among the products, the gifts, of the small bookstore. We put those *after you*s and such, those *lemme grab it for you*s and such, in the satchels of our hearts. Though it was a little place (a packed little place), I meandered, I got lost, I got found, I got lost again. I guarantee you there were nooks I had not yet discovered. (Nota bene: A good bookstore is also a nookstore, a store of nooks, inside of which await what you cannot begin to know.)

Also, and crucially, and delightfully, a staff that could answer the hell out of your questions, which I will go ahead and declare a quality, a bounty, a beauty, of the small independent bookstore: people who know their shit and are glad to share it. The last time I was in there, I was looking for W. E. B. Du Bois's *Black Reconstruction*, a book I wish I had read when it was assigned to me in college. Lots of those books. No regrets, no regrets. When I asked, the twenty-something woman working behind the counter hopped off her stool and walked directly to the floor-to-ceiling shelf across the way and pulled the Du Bois from the shelf, placing the tome and, it's not too much to say, my life, in my hands, again and again they do, these booksellers, these guides, these friends, smiling: *Here it is*.

(May 23)

62. The Door

ALWAYS AT THE DOORSTEP, I was not quite thinking, looking at Jerry's sunken eyes, his mouth slightly open, his skeleton visible beneath his skin like wax paper, like parchment, nearly translucent, luminous with the light of dying, which, too, is living, living acutely, which we're all always doing, though needing teachers sometimes to show us. The few times Jerry opened his eyes, they were like a baby's, in the vague and general direction of whatever he was looking at, or for, usually his beloved, Anne Marie. And in the depth of his resting—for that's what maybe he's doing now, resting up, getting ready—he scratched his face precisely the way he did ten, twenty years ago, which Stephanie noted and imitated with a precision that kind of shocked me:

hand open, the index finger gently itching the parchment skin beneath his eye, or the crease where his nose meets his cheek.

The second time he stirred, maybe the third, he seemed to see and recognize Stephanie, who was a kind of daughter to him—oh boy they could get into it, it was so fun; there's a story about them fighting, like really wrestling, over a telephone, but that's for another time. He reached his hand to her—his left; he, too, was a lefty—and laid his gauzy gaze upon her. Cirrus gaze. Threshold gaze. Gaze of being at the door, maybe—the door beginning to take you in. Which is also like a baby's gaze: at the beginning of something unlike anything you've seen before. Anne Marie was smiling and talking to him at the foot of the bed, gently rubbing his feet and shins, asking him again and again if it felt okay, if it felt good, preparing him, helping him, for when he's ready, to walk through.

(May 26)

63. The Minor Cordiality

THERE IS A species of human I so adore, I realized, *I felt*, as I drove today by an old farmhouse on the corner of the bottom of a big hill, and the species of human in this case was in the shape of a big burly fella in overalls with long stringy hair and a bountiful beard, who, leaning forward on his rocking chair, tossed a wave at me in the shape of a peace sign, along with a little butterfly of a smile. It might be this minor cordiality—waving from the porch at, I'm presuming, whoever goes by; I'm telling you, the ease and skill with which he dispatched his wares made me feel like it was his vocation, his calling—so warms my heart today in part because just a few days ago, not a hundred yards away on this very road, heading to the same place, I passed someone who seemed like a volunteer fireman—pickup truck with magnet light on top flashing, meant, I would learn, to dissuade anyone from continuing, though since he was parked on the side of the road, I thought it meant caution, not stop.

I kept going until I heard him start yelling and saw him in my rear-view waving me back, and when I got back to him, he leaned into my window, his Kids "Я" Us badge dangling from his lanyard, and he asked me, sort of excited, imitating the question cops love to ask when they pull you over—cops love our documents; and though the syllogism might not exactly hold, I'll offer it anyway: if we give a shit about documents, we, too, are cops—where I was going in such a hurry. By the fourth time he asked, smiling now as he was, titillated it seemed at this meager scrap of power, though I didn't see it with my own eyes, I wouldn't have been surprised if he had an erection. A chubby at least. *Where you going in such a hurry?!* Which seemed irrelevant to his duty of alerting people to the accident ahead, and that we'd have to go another way. I do not have to tell you, and I am not the first one to say so, but a badge will fuck you up. Whether it's this guy's plastic one or someone else's aluminum one or the color of our skin or our testicles or how much money we make or the language we speak or our citizenship of a given—duh, *this*—country, our badges fuck us up royally. I don't care who we think we are. (#unbadge)

Anyhow, after I grumbled, *I'm going to the supermarket*, I spent the next two hours fantasizing that I'd said *none of your goddamned business* or *eat me* or *your momma's*, and because I didn't say any of those things, I was stuck also fantasizing about mauling this dude, who, from this angle, looked to me like the second-string center on my 1990 JV football team: yanking his badge from his milky neck, slinging him to the ground, stomping him a little bit (I don't actually know if you can "stomp a little bit"), and, as he's crawling away, like a cherry on top, out of a Cormac McCarthy novel, asking him where *he's* going so fast.

Friends, here's the thing: I've spent a good while, not inordinate but far more than the allotted thirty minutes in which I try to corral these thoughts (first draft, yes), trying to get my head around this not quite blow-offable rage, so fully formed, so embodied, hair-trigger you might say—even if the trigger is on a rage that stays most often pointed inward—that it seems to come from the long memory, *epigenetic* seems again the right word, of badged motherfuckers telling my folks where they can be, and where they can't, what they can do, and what they can't—this neighborhood, this pool, this sidewalk, this restaurant, this water fountain, this college, this church, this movie theater, this basketball court, this job, this stage, this hospital, this relationship, this land, this life—all of which seems useful rage to contemplate, *critical rage* I've heard it called, though needful rage I might say, too, particularly as it helps us imagine abolishing the conditions by which the rage came to pass rather than take ownership of the conditions and inflicting them on someone else; particularly if the rage does not become the ground of our gathering, and our imagining, and our dreaming, as it has threatened to do here. If the rage is not its own objective. By which I mean, if the rage is a bridge to love.

There is a reason an alternative title for this book is *The Book of Despites*.

In addition to the porch-wavers and their ilk (the hat-tippers, the head-nodders, the thumbs-uppers and fist-pumpers) are whoever makes it their business, often (but by no means only) people working in diners, post offices, laundromats, cafés, supermarkets, bookstores, bakeries, train stations, etc., to call us *baby*, or *babe*, or *honey*, or *sweetheart*, or *love*. There are angels in this world who call people they don't know *love*. Some of them, and this makes my heart a flock of giraffes, a gaggle of manatees, are like twenty years old! *Sugar* sometimes, too, people say. Along with *pal* or *cousin* or *brother* or *youngblood* or, here in Indiana, and this I had to check wasn't fightin' words, for I'm really not from here, *bub. Bub* means "pal"; it means "friend." Or *what's good*, which might be one of the subtitles of this book of despites. And who, in the busy café (or bakery or Vietnamese joint or pizzeria or library), seeing you seeing there are no more seats, invites you to sit at their table, simply by pointing or moving their stuff or pushing the chair out with their foot, and probably smiling. Who smiles at you. And who lets you merge when you're driving, and who holds the door at the elevator. Who asks, *Could you use this?* And who stays with you when they see you need help. And who tracks you down to give you the wallet you left on the train. And who helps when your doggie takes off. And who swipes you in when they see your ticket's not working. And who stops when you blow a tire, or the radiator's shot. And who gives directions when you ask. And who walks you there.

(May 30)

64. Small Fluffy Things

I AM SORRY to report that I am not particularly sentimental or romantic about small things, all small things cute, you know that disease. I wonder if my aversion is because I was never particularly a small thing, born big and mostly stayed that way, and naturally, wanting to be cute, never got quite to be—I'll spare you that rumination and take it up in therapy. Nor am I particularly sentimental or romantic about the parent/child relationship or endeavor. I don't think I am, anyway. Interested, but you know, not extra gooey about it. Maybe more baffled and shruggy or something. I'll spare you that fib—or, more accurately, crock—and take it up in therapy.

All of that said—by the way: the preamble, I am realizing, often delights me; how long a person can avoid saying the thing they are intending to say; whether it's to contextualize or rationalize or preemptively judge (*this is only a first draft*, *I'm still working this out*, etc.); indeed, so often the preamble (the before walk: delight!) is as interesting as the walk itself; I find it to be the case often enough with my own essays, my own attempts, that I think a fun book to write would be *The Book of Preambles*; the book of putting on your socks and tying up your shoes, and if you're the type, filling up your water bottle and doing some light stretching, but skipping the walk (the essay or poem) entirely; likewise, *The Book of Digressions*, which you might call this—there was what appeared to be a family of geese traveling down the canal. Two big ones—I did not check their undersides—and five little ones, *gosling* is the word for them, named after an actor who, though handsome, is actually more cute, just like these petite, puffy creatures, who are paddling like hell to keep up with the big ones, but, just like the young among we humans, are quite distractable, hopping out of the water to poke around on the banks of the canal, or jamming their little (soft?) beaks in-between some of the smooth rocks. All is a mystery to them, a wonder, it seems. And the big geese just wait, paddling elegantly, invisibly, against the soft current, with remarkable patience it seems to me, never jangling their keys or looking at their watches. Perhaps, like me, they're thinking little other than *holy shit how cute that little guy is.* Holy shit how soft and cuddly rooting around there in the weeds, acquainting their little bodies with the trillion mysteries of the earth.

It is one hell of a trick making those little goslings—geese and humans alike—so cute, so fucking adorable, for I think that image must implant in the brains and hearts (hearts and minds) of the bigger ones, so that forever in some not very remote corner, no matter what we do, there's a picture of us fluffy and soft and wonderstruck and vulnerable to the hard edges of the world, and so, for them, you would do anything.

(June 1)

65. *Riiiiiita, Riiiiiiita!*

BECAUSE I AM sometimes inclined to forget that people, including myself, all the time have their lost things returned to them—wallets, credit cards, phones, notebooks—it is easy to look at the Xeroxed sign I saw today stapled to a phone pole a couple blocks down, which says, in a slightly frantic handwritten script, accompanying a very cuddly if oddly seductive photograph

LOST!!!

OUR BELOVED KITTY HERCULES

IF YOU SEE HIM

PLEASE CALL THIS NUMBER

(POSSIBLE REWARD)

as a futile prayer to a cruel, mewling universe rife with lost kitties and indifferent humans. Which is a kind of faith, and given as our faith predicts in no small measure how we behave, perhaps this explains why I have a few times been a careless, indifferent asshole when my friends have lost their kitties. Faith in the cruel, mewling universe has inclined me to chip into that sad place, and be like, *bummer dude.* (I'm sorry.) Just as faith in the kind, mewling universe, when I have it, inclines me to chip into that one. I'm pretty sure this is true.

Which, for the record, like everything else good in my life, I did not come to on my own. This I came to, or was brought to, as it pertains to the lost kitty signs anyway, by Kayte, whose beloved cat Rita, who purrs like a lawnmower and bashes her muscular head into your shins, a few years back one day bolted from the not-all-the-way-latched kitty carrier when they arrived at the vet's parking lot. Freaked out, Rita booked behind the plaza into the brambles back there, fleeing deeper in when Kayte came running after her. After a while, Kayte went home, made posters like these (a little shinier, truth be told; Kayte's a designer), and plastered them on phone poles throughout the surrounding neighborhoods.

Later, having learned that cats sometimes emerge from hiding at dawn and dusk, Kayte pulled her Toyota into the parking lot of the plaza in the morning dark, as the black sky had just started going blue in the east. As she walked past the vet's office, past the dumpsters out back, and into the scraggly field beyond, she started hearing what sounded like birds cooing her kitty's name: *Riiiiiita, Riiiiiiita.* She attributed it to being a little bit nervous in this dark field alone, or disoriented maybe, and then she heard the birds again: *Riiiiiiita, Riiiiiita.* But as the sun came up, silhouetting the trees in the east and glistening the dew-wet brambles, she could see it was not birdsong out there, or not only, for there were people, a handful of them, answering her prayers, or trying to, anyway.

(June 5)

66. Hands for Carrying

MY AUNT VERNA, the youngest of that hale and hearty generation, has died at ninety, and though death is sometimes a mercy, it doesn't mean the atmosphere has not fundamentally changed for the bereaved, which perhaps explains her youngest up there in the front row gasping and moaning for his mother in repose about six feet in front of him. Both of his sons lean their heads on his broad and shuddering shoulders, and from the pew behind them his big cousin, who is significantly smaller than him, with her head down, rubs his neck and the base of his skull, which evens out his breathing some. My Aunt Butter is up there looking a little extra frail, go figure. This is Butter's second sister gone in a few months, as Verna followed right behind their big sister Thelma, which probably she did, too, when they were kids, and which I witnessed her do when people were giving testimonials at my own father's memorial, where Nana, feeling perhaps a little under-acknowledged (as was her way; as is a lot of our ways), stood up and said to the gathered, *I'm the momma, I'm the one who beat him*. After Nana sat down, Aunt Verna gave her a generous beat, then stood up and recited the William Ernest Henley poem "Invictus," which she said, with some pride, my father also knew by heart.

From the back of the church, I was studying the stained-glass Jesus, who looked like a William H. Johnson or Jacob Lawrence painting. From all the shadows I guess he could have been an Alice Neel Jesus, too. Probably because we were a mostly black congregation, I spent a little time, as a way perhaps to hear less the moaning, trying to ascertain if the Jesus looking down on us was a white Jesus, or a light-skinned black Jesus, or a swarthy Semitic Jesus. Though I can't say for sure, it is undisputable how big were his feet and hands, and how sturdy. Feet for walking. Hands for carrying. And, depending on the sun, how from time to time they glowed.

(June 11)

67. Mulberry Picking

YOU WANT TO get your garlic in by Halloween. Your peas by St. Paddy's. Where I live, forsythia is one of the first bloomers, maybe the first yellow thing, and some people say those fiery flowers are the cue to prune your apples and pears. The last frost here is May 15, maybe these days a little sooner, and if you test it, praying your tomatoes and peppers and okra into the garden in late April, or mid, giddy for summer, poor thing, a freeze will bite your sweet little ass. Anyway, it was to this earthly metronome I realized, a few years back, walking through town on June 13 and spotting a purple splotched sidewalk, that the mulberry trees fruit, are in the early midst of their fruiting, on this, my father's birthday. It was the kind of grand realization, a wondrous confluence of beloveds—my father and mulberries; my father yearly resurrected as the mulberries; my father and sweetness and abundance and nourishment and joy—that made so much heart-healing cosmic sense that you'd never in a million years forget it.

But I would, I learned today, shortly after finding a place to sit outside the little café whose theme, it seems, is pot—like marijuana, weed, bud, grass, ganja, etc. There was lots of CBD this and that, and the place had a vaguely hydroponic feel. Air plants and plants stuffed into canvas bags and planting medium (neither of which are hydroponic, I know) looking beneath their trippy fluorescent lights sickly desperate for real soil. I got my espresso in a glass (espresso in a glass: delight!), grabbed a seat at the wobbly table outside, and was reminded how much I love the unwobbly table, which I DIY'd with a shim of napkins. And sipping my glass of espresso, I spotted across the parking lot in the woods a tree whose shiny leaves beckoned, and because you sure as shit need to heed the beckoning of trees, I heeded, with my glass of espresso, across the lot to the woods where, you have already figured this out, yup, there was a fruiting mulberry tree. And after plucking and savoring as many of the sweet black fruit as I could reach—the unforgettable edible cosmic bells of my father's birth, you remember—then sitting back down at my newly shimmed table, then looking at my stupid alienation machine (cellular telephone), which is also a calendar (and a calculator!), and seeing the date, I thought, *Whoa, I forgot, it's Dad's birthday! Happy birthday, Dad!*

And though remembering it's my old man's birthday, especially almost-but-not-exactly by virtue of picking and munching mulberries, is a delight indeed, it's not today's delight of record. (*Sorry, Dad!*) Or not solely anyway: to be sure, the day my dad was born, and my mom for that matter, and their moms and dads, and theirs, when I'm glad to be alive anyway, is the first delight of record. That would be zillions of delights of record, by the way.

Today's (other) delight of record is the simple act of plucking small ripe fruit, which I was doing while holding my glass of espresso, pushing branches from my face and blinking sometimes hard to keep those branches from blinding me, a mindbogglingly athletic feat of proprioception we do not often enough shout out, far as I'm concerned. That any of us can manipulate our thumbs and fingers in this way, often while reaching on our tippy-toes, is really freaky. The opposable thumb with which to grasp but mostly not smash. The eyes with which to focus on one pulse of sweet black in the mulberry fathoms. Which is itself enough, far as I'm concerned. That's like a triple-decker delight right there. But then you remember all that agile plucking, all that harvest, all that desire for sweetness, connects you to the bears and raccoons and deer and possums and squirrels and ants and blue jays and crows, not to mention all those moms and dads of moms and dads who so kindly got born (*Happy Birthday, Dad!*) and so many of whom have done the very same thing you are doing right now—maybe sans the espresso—which might be a nice thing to remember the next time you're feeling lonely, the next time you've been convinced you're alone.

(June 13)

68. Garlic Harvest (NC-17)

I MENTIONED ALREADY the realization I've had this year that every time I plant garlic, or any seed really—like every time—though I expect it to come up (from experience, it most always does), I am always elated, and sort of bamboozled, that it actually does. A little bit, if not on the outside then on the inside, I do backflips. Lots of internal *holy shit*–ing. This happy realization does not stop, I learned today, with the seed sprouting, the garlic sending their little green periscopes up, but continues all the way to the harvest, which I did today by myself because Stephanie is out of town and it's a root day on the biodynamic calendar, which we pretty much go by.

Here's a little garlic thing: shortly before it's time to harvest, maybe a month or six weeks, the hardneck variety sends up its seedheads, which you may have encountered at a farmer's market or fancy restaurant by the name of *scapes*. You've maybe had them roasted or sauteed or in a salad or, if you're real fancy, in a pesto. Scapes are sort of a bonus food, a delicacy of excess, because, since the scape will become the flower, which is the plant's attempt to reproduce, which it really wants to do (the plant at this time is kind of in rut, kind of in high school), you snap or snip them if you want the bulb to get as big and swollen as it can. The better to eat.

All that said, because Stephanie and I had both been gone for a spell, the scapes got ahead of us, randy as they were for some botanical nookie. When I got home, I saw that some of the seedheads were bulging from their sheaths. So I went around snapping the scapes, which were thicker and harder than when I usually pluck them, and while I was doing so I prayed that they hadn't sucked all the juice from the swelling roots, which I wouldn't find out for another ten days or so, when it was harvest time. When the time came, I was nervous, convinced the bulbs would be puny, that I'd messed it up. But the first one I pulled, which lifted easily from the friable soil threaded with mycelium, was a pretty good size. The next one, too, whoa, pretty good.

On it went, each time a quiver of nervousness, a flicker of anticipatory disappointment, and almost to a one the heads came out big and firm, following which a little sigh of relief, or, often, a gasp or cheer or some rooting at how big the bulbs. (I do a good bit of rooting in the garden.) By the time I gathered up all the piles of garlic and spread them out in the screened-in porch where they'll cure for the next several weeks, the biggest pile of garlic we've ever grown, the biggest haul I'd ever seen from such a little garden, I started laughing and laughing and, for some reason I'm not quite sure of, I kind of can't stop.

(June 26)

69. Sunflower in the Mortar

IN AN ALMOST uncanny feat of symmetry, another affirmation of the palindromic world, the world circling around to catch itself, the world a flummoxment of beauty bells ringing in your every periphery, Stephanie and I noticed, walking in Bloomington down Belton Way—almost directly across from the butterfly bush that emits the world's most wig-flippingest smell outside Don's old house and that has been, the past couple weeks, flipping my wig—a sunflower growing out of a crack in the mortar between two huge limestone blocks of the wall—a WPA project, the plaque says—around Rose Hill Cemetery. How reasonable, if you're going to have a thing called a country (not a given), to have also a thing called a WPA, or any number of other things aside from a military, that pay people decently and make things work better. A trillion dollars yearly into the war industry, or a trillion dollars into jobs planting trees and replacing the lead pipes and reriveting the bridges and putting in the high-speed trains already and beautifying the schools and paying the teachers well and building limestone walls around the cemeteries. Seems a no-brainer to me, but I'm just a poet. I'm a flower guy.

Despite which, we almost walked right by this one, which was still, I'd say, in early adolescence, before the first flowers were beginning to form. I can't remember who, but one of us noticed, stopped, grabbed the other's arm, like, "Is that . . .?" We both laughed and shook our heads no, meaning "yes," meaning "impossible but indeed"—how often, perhaps most often, delight is shown to you by someone tugging your arm; how often, perhaps most often, delight makes you want to tug someone's arm. We inspected the tiny buds at the top, the reddish, furry stem, the tiny crack it grew from in the mortar in the wall that was, at the very most, I mean the complete, total, fulsome, absolute very most, the size of a sunflower seed. Maybe a little smaller. It was the kind of crack that, if you were a layperson inspecting the mortar, maybe even not a layperson, you'd think almost nothing of it, and certainly wouldn't think it needed pointing.

So how did it get there, we wondered, and surmised that, among the possibilities, the most likely was that a sparrow or finch stashed it there, or squirreled it away maybe more apt, finched it away even more, and came back some weeks later for a snack to find now a flower. Or a flower soon to be (and, incidentally, in a few more weeks, a much bigger snack). Or who knows, maybe the bird thought a sunflower would look nice right here, can't hurt to try—this is not unthinkable to me, given as the goldfinches planted all of the sunflowers in our yard with what I would call superb design sensibility. So good, pedestrians often come through our alley to admire their work, attributing it to us.

But it also has to be noted—remembered—that this was not a garden, no soil or woodchips or compost or goat poo. Not even a little sludge or leaf litter or gravel. This was a sunflower growing out of a crack in a rock. A smidge of rain and light. If you're thinking it's a little bit of a cliché, all the obvious and potent meanings, survival despite the harshness, resilience, making a way out of no way, the fugitive seed finding a patch of survivable earth, etc., yeah, I guess so. But more I'm thinking the unlikely collaborations by which we come to pass at all, any of us, the trillions and trillions, the literal trillions and trillions, to the bottom of which we will never, lord let us, get.

(July 3)

70. Yellowjackets

I WAS SITTING on the porch this morning as it was warming up and I noticed the yellowjackets just beyond the arugula and squash ascending from the log they're living in, heading out for work it looks like. Teeny lunch pails in wing. Sometimes they look like embers lifting from a fire. They're a comfortable distance away, maybe ten or twelve feet, and I rarely think anything of them unless someone comes over with a dog or a kid, in which case I say, *Don't go near the log, there's yellowjackets in there.* Sometimes we're quiet for a few beats, the human eyes adjust and see our busy little neighbors, and then all is copacetic. One time I was strolling around my garden with a militant vegan friend who noticed a few yellowjackets digging into a dropped pear and told me unironically that I needed to find their home and incinerate them right away. That we must preemptively obliterate whatever might possibly sting us. Or we could not.

(July 4)

71. The Courtesy of Truckers

I GOT CAUGHT having to pee pretty bad with no exit or rest stop in sight, and so I pulled over on the side of the busy highway with a rather petite shoulder, and as I was relieving myself, intermittently watching the plants shivering on the side of the road and the traffic roaring by over my shoulder, I noticed how every single trucker (this was a trucker-rich road), by which I mean *every single one*, managed their rigs over to the passing lane, and some of them, because it was a busy road, had to do so nimbly, balletically, all to give me and my relief a little breathing room. The trucker's quick and urgent wide berth for the shouldered car, which might also be a shouldered truck or tractor trailer or someone being pulled over or an ambulance, reminds me of the way in some of the mosh pits I'd be in back in the day—Fugazi, Shudder to Think, Rage Against the Machine, Fishbone; Fishbone eight, maybe ten times; Fishbone today if I could get a ticket—where if someone went down, you immediately scooped them to their feet, and made sure they were okay (eye contact, hand signals, thumbs ups, or any of the zillion other ways humans can communicate *I'm good* and *thank you* to one another), and if you were on the other side of the pit you immediately went from moshing to boxing out your fellow moshers so no one got stomped, never mind most moshers back in the day (some of them probably on anti-jock principle) did not know what boxing out meant. Regardless, when someone went down, they boxed out like Dennis Rodman or Charles Barkley. Truckers are also really astute at flashing their lights to oncoming traffic to mean *heads up cop* or *heads up accident* or *heads up washing machine* or *heads up family of deer meandering cutely in the middle of the road.* Those flashing lights are another kind of boxing out, I guess.

Additionally, for the most part truckers—who, lest we forget, keep everything going; i.e., thank a trucker—know not to gum up the passing lane, and when they are gumming it up and you're just starting to get frustrated and itchy and thinking *what the hell are they doing up there* and *time to pull your head outta your ass, bozo,* you'll see a sign, often blinking, the better to alert you to yourself, that says *Truckers Left Lane Only.* Very occasionally, at night, when I'm tired but with miles to go before I sleep, I'll let myself slip into the fantasy that a truck behind me is a demon truck, like that Stephen King movie, and let it be said that Stephen King kinda ruined a lot of shit. Tell me you wouldn't be afraid to stay the winter for free in a big beautiful empty ski lodge with lots of food and these days probably Wi-Fi and a pool. Tell me you're not a little bit afraid of home-coming or prom or whatever. Tell me you're not a little bit afraid of big cuddly slobbery dogs, or clowns, or '57 Chevys, or cornfields, or your pets, or your kids. See what I'm saying?

Anyway, as far as I know, it hasn't happened yet, the demon truck thing, but something that happens frequently, particularly if I have extended a courtesy to a truck, by which I mean a trucker—maybe I let them in front of me in the left lane when we're climbing a hill because the truck in front of them in the right was really huffing and puffing; maybe I let them in as the road went from three lanes to two, or two lanes to one—that trucker, if it's nighttime, once you get back in front of them, will often flip their lights on and off a few times in a gesture that, the first time it happened to me, I thought maybe I'd messed up and I was being reprimanded and oh god I hope I didn't just sic the demon truck on myself. But now I know it's an acknowledgment of my unremarkably good deed. It's yet another way we have of saying thank you.

(July 7)

72. *How Literature Saved My Life*

SHORTLY BEFORE DAWN I slid out of bed and crept to the other room to reread, or re-reread, David Shields's book *How Literature Saved My Life*, which I first read in 2013, staying the year with Stephanie and her family back in Frenchtown, New Jersey. At the time I was working on, or trying to anyway, a serious, historical, journalistic, and authoritative book. I was jotting down facts and figures, trying to *mortar* the knowledge I was acquiring into an unbreachable argument, a thesis in fact, that would, in addition to money and prizes and stuff, no joke, get me invited on the shows as an "expert." And you won't believe this: I was not enjoying myself.

Around this time I was browsing a bookstore—by the way, among my favorite activities, wandering through other people's minds, especially if it's a bookshop whose curation I love, where it's wandering through the writers' *and* booksellers' minds, a kind of polyamorous nerdiness—and I stumbled upon Shields's book, outward facing and accompanied by a handwritten lovenote from one of the booksellers. As I made my way through it, in addition to the short entries, the humor, the digressions and associations, I noticed that though it is taut with an almost athletic readerliness—dude reads everything and clearly knows a ton (stuff is kind of oozing out of dude's ears)—the book seems more interested in inexpertise than expertise. (For the expert of the expertly inexpert, the Michael Jordan or the Roger Federer of it, see Geoff Dyer.) Or maybe a better way to say it: the book is very curious. In fact, maybe you'd call it a book of curiosity about his curiosity: about his almost doppelganger, the writer Ben Lerner; about his growing up an athlete and a nerd; about his speech impediment; about love and sex and relationships; about writing and writers and books. All of which points toward my favorite curiosity of all: why we are who we are.

Which, at least if we go hard—by which I really mean if we try to be honest—is complicated, and probably a little bit destabilizing, for being curious about oneself (just as being curious about someone else), which means trying to know oneself, requires as well, and crucially, that we be willing to unknow ourselves (T-shirt: *Unknow Thyself!*), which always seems to me, but maybe a little extra done in public, or in the kind of public a book might be, roooouuuuggggghhhh, in no small part because we are, most of us anyway, many, many things, including—and this the honest curiosity might reveal—unadmirable. By which I more maybe mean *broken*. Unheroically, unovercomingly so.

Though not only broken, for the unknowing of oneself—also known as *wonder*ing about oneself, in the mind the page sometimes makes—is also like walking through a city you do not quite know, following a scent or a sound or a group of people or traveling through an alley that bends toward what might be, well, who knows? *Erotic* is the word I don't think Christopher Alexander and them use in *A Pattern Language*, but they might as well have. Shields seems to know this, which is why, too, *How Literature Saved My Life* almost exudes self-pleasure. The wondering, the wandering around inside oneself, is not a little bit auto-erotic. Or, let's just say *fun*, so the children can stay in the room. This was a book that seemed, seems, like it might have been fun to write.[1]

Which was not yet quite an idea in my head. Duty,

1 While revising this I happened to read Lydia Davis's brief writerly coming-of-age essay "A Beloved Duck Gets Cooked: Forms and Influences I," where she describes a similar experience, which makes me wonder if, though it kind of took the top of my head off, this realization that writing can be enjoyable is not all that uncommon among writers.

obligation, calling, vocation; burden, slog, miserable, and sometimes—though when I said this last one out of my mouth in front of a class I was assisting him in teaching, the poet Alan Shapiro kindly disabused me of the notion by asking me if I'd ever been waterboarded—*torture*. But fun? Writing *fun*? And this is how *How Literature Saved My Life* saved my life, my writing life anyway: by showing me I might enjoy this work, even when—as I sometimes find myself while doing it, this unknowing myself—shedding actual tears out of my very eyes.

(July 11)

73. Hickies, Ostentatiously Blandished

THOUGH THERE IS something so, umm, weird to me about the way the children these days unabashedly flaunt their hickies like they're jewelry or something, how they almost wear them like a fleeting public emblem—a bruisy ring I guess—of having been Hoovered for a night or afternoon or something, that doesn't mean I don't like it. I mean I like it on their behalf, I like it for them, I like that these kids have apparently kicked the hickey shame. (I know shame is like water and just looks for a place to settle, but still, sometimes it's nice even to celebrate when shame moves someplace else.) I remember the ends to which so many of my generation went trying to conceal their welts (comb, ice, etc.). The ends to which I went concealing any possibility of being a desirous creature from my parents or any of the adults in my midst, etc. (Oh, I just remembered this: if a woman ballpark my mother's age was working the counter of CVS when I was getting my condoms, I'd bail, or sometimes just steal them.) The miserable internal chatter that goes along with that shame, the beliefs, the wreckage. Not these kids. Not hickey shame anyway. As I was drinking a coffee on the porch of the café and watched a few of their bruised ilk go unselfconsciously by, I breathed an actual sigh of relief. *How nice*, I thought.

When I was but a young professor of poetry, an assistant as it's called on the inside, which means on six years' probation, a six-year tryout, six years pretending you agree with everyone and doing any-and-everything asked of you, a student once came to my office with so many goddamned hickies on his neck, I mean it was hickies on top of hickies, it was so many hickies they made a kind of Joan Mitchell painting of his throat, a purple swarm of untentacled jellyfish wrapped about his pale neck, slurping from the neck of his T-shirt up to about the fine hairs of his chin. These adamant hickies, which one might in a corny way say were like a map of desire, were like a map of how this kid had been almost eaten, looked like to me. I worked as hard as I ever have not to let my eyes drift down from his eyes to his collar, where he looked around the neck like an albino leopard or something. Dude was so bruised up, and because it was a full fifteen years before these new heroic shameless hickey hussies, his being unconcealed made me think *maybe this is a plea for help. Maybe I am supposed to liberate this kid from some suction dungeon*, while answering to the best of my ability his questions about line breaks in Theodore Roethke and why we were watching Richard Pryor videos in a poetry class.

But given as I was still on probation and inclined to keep my job, in addition to always keeping my door open and other such ancillary self-policings, I went the extra mile in adhering to all of the possible prohibitions, ultimately, on closeness, on taking care, because there is an office for that and it is not this one, put it on your syllabus, that's not your job, and I understand how closeness easily teeters or spills into abuse especially where power is unequally distributed, where the hierarchical power structure is the bedrock of the system, or rather, it *is* the system, and the first and almost sole lesson of school is the preservation of that hierarchical power structure, but isn't it interesting, no, I mean *sad*, isn't it sad, that rather than troubling or even eliminating the power structure and thereby the inevitable, the *requisite* abuse of power, we excise the closeness, or the possibility of such, we preserve the power at the expense of closeness, keeping, always, our distance, for which, in this instance anyway, thank god, because it kept me from blurting out what I was thinking though I kinda knew the answer ballpark, too: *Dude, what happened to your neck?!*

(July 12)

74. Dream Redux

LAST NIGHT I dreamt I was taking my mother to what I knew was a great little restaurant, the kind of spot I love and figured she would, too, quirkily dinery, with a very good veggie burger and fries. Unlike how this dream usually goes—I'm driving back and forth on some streets looking up a hill or wandering a market knowing the best veggie burger and fries are around here somewhere; or I drive by where I'm pretty sure it is but I'm running late and don't have time to dillydally—we had time to dillydally, and I knew exactly where the spot was. But when we started walking there—I had been talking this place up to my mom for a while—I realized, looking around, oh, this is kind of a seedy area, lots of sex shops, some drug stuff going on. I walked a little closer to my mom, who didn't seem to notice, and when we finally got off the street and into the spot, I realized I had forgotten that my favorite veggie burger and fries place was in the back room of a sex shop. Not like a porn shop. A shop for having sex. I can't quite track my thinking in the dream—though in nondream life I'd happily eat a good veggie burger and french fries in the back of a sex shop, I would *never* take my mother to do so, no matter how good the fries—I'm assuming I thought the food was so good that it was worth it, and that we'd be quickly taken to the restaurant part of the shop, and maybe that, since it was daytime, afternoon, the perverts would be sleeping still. Perverts and vampires.

But as we were waiting, I heard some moaning and I noticed a couple behind my mother teetering on bar stools masturbating each other, and then I looked around and realized we were surrounded by what seemed like a fornicatory soiree. When I realized that I had inadvertently brought my mother to an orgy, I barked to her, "Ma, get out of here!" I took her by the elbow and gave her a shove, yelling *Go!*, which I feel bad about because she's eighty-one years old, but I had to. It must have been one of those scenes where you sometimes pay different attention to something because you're in the presence of, and paying attention to, someone else who's now paying attention to it. My favorite example is the time Stephanie and I were listening to Maggie Nelson's book *The Argonauts* while driving across the country with her daughter Georgia who was plugged into her own alienation machine in the back seat, listening to music and sleeping, but every single time she'd take her headphones off to say something to us, Maggie Nelson would mention ass-fucking. Though we'd already read the book at that point probably three times, we heard it newly with the seventeen-year-old girl riding in the backseat.

When we finally ran out of the sex shop/veggie burger joint, the throbbing music growing quieter behind us, we made our way into a kind of plaza, the kind of plaza you might find in the Basque Country, or maybe Barcelona, and we quickly came upon a restaurant that seemed just so-so to me, but my mom grabbed one of the paper menus pinched between the salt and pepper shakers, said, *Huh they have cinnamon sugar toast,* and maybe no longer trusting my taste, said, *I think I'd like to eat here.*

(July 13)

75. Angels All

I PICKED UP a guy named Stan who was looking for one of the homeless shelters today—actually, he asked me if I knew where the shelter was, and I told him yes, did my best to explain to him where it was—go up here three long blocks to Third, make a left, dogleg to stay on third, then you'll walk about a mile, pass a donut shop, a dogleg into . . . etc.—then I got into my car to drive home, which is in the exact direction of where Stan was heading. I wasn't wanting to be bothered, I thought, looking into my rearview mirror as I was pulling out. I heard myself think it like this: *Aw man, I don't want to be bothered today.* Then I said to myself, as I saw him picking up his big bag to hoof it the two or so miles on this ninety-degree day, *You asshole, ask him if he wants a ride*, which he did, apologizing that he didn't have any money to give me. I convinced him it was okay, I was good, then he hopped in, keeping his big bag with him in the front seat, sort of squished. When he heard the car start complaining about the seatbelt, he buckled up.

When I asked him where he was from, he said, "Kentucky, sir," although it was clear to me, and I'd assume him, too, that we were about the same age, which was borne out when he told me his birthday was a week after mine, and he'd be turning fifty—a couple years my senior was Stan. A long row to hoe though, sounded like, because he was just released from the psych ward—I've heard it maybe called the third floor in our town?—for trying to kill himself, I didn't catch the method. Though he told me he'd also tried hanging himself, and one time when the voices were really bad he got a motel room and put a shotgun in his mouth, pulled the trigger, but it didn't go off—until he set it down on the bed, where it blew a hole through the wall. He started crying a little bit at the prospect of it having hit someone else, hurting or killing them. *I'd've been locked up for life*, he said, wiping his eyes. He so badly wanted to make his daughters and grandkids proud, he said, before telling me how worried his daughters were. *They're so scared.*

When we pulled up to the first shelter, he looked around, and seeing the guys milling around, said *Oh no, I don't think this is the one, but that's okay, I can get out*, opening the door. *Well let's find another one,* I said, and he closed the door, his big bag still on his lap, and told me again he wished he had money to give me, then, pointing at some shrubs along the busy road said, *I'd rather sleep in them bushes right there than in that shelter.* I looked at the little Xerox of the map he was given at the hospital, realized the shelter he wanted was very near where we started out, so we started back-tracking. As we were passing Kroger he took a call, which I assume was from a caseworker, and she told him his tests all came back negative. He started crying again and said, *Thank you ma'am I'm gonna do right* and such. Then he told me he was so happy and broke up a little more. I dropped him off at the other shelter, which he thanked me for, tearing up again, then he read that the shelter wasn't open until the next morning, but he said he'd sleep right there. I said, *Are you sure?* He said, *Yes* and *I'll be fine* and *bless you* and such. I pulled a few bucks out of my pocket for him, and said here, take this, which, again, made him tear up, and tell me, again, *If you give me your address, I get paid every month*, etc. *I'm good*, I told him again.

I pulled away and thought I would run back to the coffee shop where I'd just had a nice conversation with a reverend in town whose work is caring for these folks.

I was going to ask where I could take Stan. But driving there down one of the roads where the homeless in our town congregate—small town, huge population of unhoused people, most of whom I drive right by, or ride my bike right by, or walk right by, feeling saintly when I give one or the other a smidgen of the cash in my pocket, feeling righteous and good—I realized there is nowhere to take him. There is nowhere to go. I drove past the park that's become a kind of shantytown with various camps set up, piles of belongings, tents, blankets, always a person or two stationed at the intersections asking for money—the park, incidentally, where the university, my current employer, which is safe bet at this very second erecting a twenty-million-dollar building, first stood. The university that pays me a lot of money, a handsome chunk of which I give (belatedly, always, admittedly) to the government who makes for goddamned sure not to divert any of it from what it's meant for, mainly the arms manufacturers and the wars they need to keep their coffers full.

By the time I got back to the house, my skin sort of crawling with what you might call a latent conscience, I was like, *You asshole he needs a place to stay*, which Stephanie of course cosigned, looking around to see how we could clean up the living room and such. But given he made it clear he really needed to sleep, and our house is little, and, truth be told, Stan seemed like he might be a late-night talker and I needed to sleep, too, I thought maybe the Hampton Inn would be better. We pulled up to the shelter, where Stan was sitting on the curb with his bag beneath his legs and asked him if that would be okay. He started crying a little bit, told Stephanie she had a good man, which I was not so sure of, before he hopped in. We talked a little bit along the way, passing the shantytown on our left, parsing out how many nights he would need until his daughter's boyfriend could get up there to bring him home. Once we checked him in and got him to his room—a big bed, air conditioner running, shades to pull tight so he could rest—he cried so hard that when he hugged Stephanie he made her neck wet, and after he hugged me and cried on my shoulder and told us he gets a check every month, etc., and we told him we're okay, etc., he told us we were angels, again and again he told us, *you all are angels.* Which I was having a hard time believing, but if he's right then angels might be we all.

(July 21)

76. Sunergos

TURNS OUT STAN'S daughter's boyfriend wasn't able to get off work, so I decided to run him down to Louisville, which worked out good for me not only because after those two hours of talking I think I have made a new friend, but also because I am writing this very delight at an outdoor table at Sunergos Coffee on Preston Street, one of my favorite cafés in the world not only for the very good coffee, the decor (i.e., comfy sofa and chairs), the not terrible music, the magazine rack, the back patio, etc., but because it is down the block from where my friends Chris and Laurel used to live, and so we spent many hours camped out here, talking shit, visiting, laughing hard enough to fall off the couch. I can hear Chris's very high, wispy laugh in there as I write this. It's like a gravelly hot air balloon. It's like one of those kites with blades on the tail. I can also hear Laurel laughing, sort of a guitar sometimes, and sometimes like a tire popping. More like a floatie, a duck-shaped floatie popping. And our friend Dave, who, though the instigator of so much of the laughter, himself has a somewhat subtle, quieter laugh—in fact the loudest, the most boisterous part of Dave's laughter is the look of gladness that comes over him when people in his midst fall to pieces. That sounds like a field of sunflowers turning toward the sun. That sounds like a generous rain. Stephanie's in there too, smiling and studying Chris and Laurel's kids who are learning how to walk and talk—and laugh, especially at Dave, whose name they say like they're bending a guitar string, whose name they say like a soft rain beginning to fall, like a sunflower craning his neck.

A dude just turned the corner of Chris and Laurel's old street and walked in this direction, and for about three or four steps, maybe five, I thought it was Chris—I even caught myself lifting my hand getting ready to yell his name. But when he got a little bit closer I saw he looked nothing like Chris. In fact, he was wearing Docksiders and khaki shorts and a polo shirt and aviator glasses, and Chris is a vans and jeans guy. Like, seriously. But you know how when you're picking someone up at the airport, especially someone you're very excited to see, someone you love, and almost every single person coming out the doors looks like who you're waiting for?

(July 23)

77. Hugging in the Co-Op

I AM PROBABLY what you'd call a game, or even enthusiastic hugger, and so the year-or-so-long prohibition on the act, you know, like for those of us who went along with those recommendations: bummer. (A bit of angelic, defiant, punk-rock graffiti that arrived in our neighborhood sometime in spring of 2020, advice I was still too terrified to take, though I was glad to know it was out there: HUG YOUR FRIENDS.) I recall the first time I hugged someone not my partner in the interim—I guess not my partner or mother or a friend who was feeling suicidal for a little while go figure and showed up on our step in obvious and dire need of a hug—was in the co-op, and when we hugged, well, let's just say my body noticed it.

And then a week or two later, during an official though short-lived reprieve from the previous year-or-so-long moratorium on hugging—before they realized not everyone was following orders and getting their shots, after which revelation the hugging had to slow down, or be only among an in-group; it was kind of like pre-*Loving* v. *Virginia* that way; hugging the wrong person would doom the race—I saw another friend, who seemed to have spent the previous year terrified, more frightened, or maybe *differently* frightened than me, but she had recently been protected and purified, and so, when she asked if I was hugging, I opened my arms and said *yup*, and we too embraced, she leaned her face against my chest, and we melted into one another. Also outside the co-op. If I were to place pins on a map of my first post-moratorium hugs, most of them would be inside or just outside the co-op. Which, for me at least, recommends the place.

Anyhow, the hug, yes, I guess that is one delight, or as many delights as there are hugs to give or receive, if you like hugs, which not everyone does. But since I do, the return of the hug for that brief spell, the reprieve from unhugging, was likewise a delight. And the next reprieve from unhugging, a delight as well. It is another example of the deprivation of the delight making the delight light harder. I mean brighter. I suspect after the next prohibition on hugs, and the lifting of the prohibition, the hugs will again be that much more delightful. Though I've made up my mind, I'm with that punk-rock graffiti; I've been terrified out of touching who I love, and who too wants to touch me, for the last time. As William Carlos Williams almost says about poetry, which I'd say is also a kind of touch: "[We] die miserably every day for lack of what is found there."

Anyway, I was in the co-op picking up a few odds and ends for dinner, and a dude with longish hair and flip-flops and a relaxed manner came up to me and held out his arms as though to hug, and when I looked puzzled, like *I don't know if I know you*, he reminded me he was the former principal of a school I've worked with, a great principal who told me at least two things that really stuck: children whose teachers believe they are going to graduate will graduate; and that he eats magic mushrooms every New Year. That's the principal I want.

I went *yo* or *hey* or something to express my happiness, which was genuine, and deep, for dude kinda changed my life—the shrooms thing less than the believing in kids thing—and then he said I want to give you a good, meaningful hug, something like that—hippy-ish, men's-groupish, untoxic masculinity-ly—and he did, it was so meaningful, his head kind of tucked into my chest, his hands on my lower and upper back, a gapless torso to torso, several long breaths worth of hug, enough hug in fact that I thought, first, *Damn, that's a lot of hug*—remember, I'm not shy this way—and second, when he wasn't letting go, I thought, *Well I guess this is what we're doing* in the avocados and onions and potatoes, I think I saw some shallots, and I kind of dug in, I relaxed into it, several more long breaths of hug, after which we had a brief but very eye-contacty conversation, still two-thirds, maybe three-quarters, arm in arm, and I remembered why I loved this dude.

(July 23)

78. Throwing Children

IT IS SOME miracle some delight when a kid who has a hard time becomes a kid who's having a good time in no small part thanks to you throwing that kid in the air again and again on a mile-long walk home from the Indian joint as her mom looks sideways at you like *you don't need to keep doing that* because you're pouring with sweat and breathing a little bit now, you're getting a good workout, but even though it's sometimes very hard for you to believe, you say *I'm good, I'm good*, because the kid laughs like a horse up there laughs like a kangaroo beating her wings against the light because she laughs like a happy little kid and when coming down and grabbing your forearm to brace herself for the time when you will drop her which you don't and slides her hand into yours as she says for the fortieth time the fiftieth time inexhaustible her delight *again again* again and again and you say *give me til the redbud tree* or *give me til the persimmon tree* because she knows the trees and so quiet you almost can't hear through her giggles she says *okay* til the next tree, when she explodes howling yanking your arm from the socket *again again* all the wolves and mourning doves flying from her tiny throat and you throw her so high she lives up there in the tree for a minute she notices the ants organizing on the bark and a bumblebee carousing the little unripe persimmon in its beret she laughs and laughs as she hovers up there like a bumblebee like a hummingbird up there giggling in the light like a giddy little girl up there the world knows how to love.

(July 24)

79. The Cave City Watermelon Festival

IT WAS MY good fortune today to have accompanied my friend Aimee to the Cave City Watermelon Festival in Arkansas. Aimee's writing a book about fruit and getting paid to do it—good work if you can get it. (Delight's not too bad either.) Since Aimee got dibs on fruit, my book in that vein will be about French fries. (Seriously.) On the beautiful drive through the rolling hills of Arkansas, because we didn't see many non-white-looking people on the website or announcements for the festival, and because, well, you know, we joked to each other that we hoped we weren't headed to a Klan rally disguised as a watermelon festival. These days when I make such jokes—which does not ungood the joke, by the way—I like to remember, by which I mean I cringe to remember, that I voted a couple years ago for an architect of the 1994 crime bill (a Yankee, by the way), by which we've come to have the largest enslaved—pardon me, I mean *incarcerated*—population on the planet. (T-shirt: *Let's Complicate Our Shit!*)

First of all, you'll be glad to know, the Cave City Watermelon Festival is in fact a watermelon festival, I was almost immediately assured, because walking from the overflow parking to the fairgrounds, I noticed a gaggle of children dressed like watermelons. Then I noticed other children dressed, if not as watermelons, at least in red. Then I noticed Aimee, too, was dressed in red—a red dress with one strap for which she received, from women, I was counting, at least three compliments—and I asked her if she was dressed for the festival. She acted a little bit like *duh, it took you long enough to notice*. It was a little chilly, and Aimee wished she had a T-shirt she could've put atop her red watermelon-themed dress, but the only one she brought was from a strawberry festival, and that, she said with conviction, would not do.

Second, I immediately spotted some brown people—when I say brown, I mean not white, or not white-looking, a population to which my eyes, especially in mostly-white or white-looking settings, are very drawn—some vendors, some parents, and some children, most of whom were being kept an eye on by whom

I'm guessing were their grandparents. One of those grandparents had a well-fitting WORLD'S BEST GRANDPA T-shirt tucked into jeans, which went along with a ball cap and cowboy boots. His curly-headed charge was right behind him, giggling and getting a bag of popcorn almost as big as he was. Grandpa and I made eyes and smiled at each other, which strikes me as a cousin of the negreeting, a kind of equation that goes something like: *If I love someone who looks like you, and you love someone who looks like me, then we might love one another.* Grandkids can be good for such math.

After stopping at a few of the vendor tents to check out the wares—Aimee got a birdhouse from a burly fella in a camo hat and jacket who was sweet as pie—we made our way past the vaccine tent to where two women were selling all kinds of brittle (peanut, cashew, pecan), which I figured I'd get for my mom, since she loves brittle. It was obviously very homemade, by which I mean made at their home as opposed to a commercial kitchen or some other certification requiring setup. Quite big Ziploc bags from which the lead woman, who I learned was the daughter, managed to offer me a sample while holding the bag in the deftest noncontamination maneuver I've ever seen. The brittle was superb, airy, a little bit different from my mother's, and we talked about how they made it. Then I saw the jams and pickles, which I learned were the mom's jam (and pickles), and we talked a bit about them: watermelon rind pickles; fig, gooseberry, and chokecherry jam. *Ooh, chokecherry*, I said. *My grampa had a chokecherry tree. Do you love it?*

I love them all, she told us from her folding chair at the back of the tent, though it seemed she was partial to gooseberry, which she told me is sweet and tart *and* delicious on biscuits, which they do good in these parts. They both smiled kind of wistfully as they described their sweet delectables, piled up all around them, telling us neither of them can eat what they make because they both have diabetes, at which point I realized what a few minutes earlier I thought was a joke about the fig jam not being good for diabetics, chuckling after they said it, was probably not. *But it sure makes us glad to know other people can*, the mother said, or the daughter, I can't remember which.

But where's the watermelon? we wondered, after we wended through the festivities the tenth time—every time with me looking to see if the funnel cake truck was open; bummer, no—until we noticed a line starting to form, a line that would eventually snake through the grounds, at the front of which was a big refrigerated truck stuffed with watermelons, and a crew of high school boys, I'll bet you they were the football team, tossing the fruits, fireman style, to the folding tables, which were wobbling some under the girth, and slicing the melons longwise into huge smiles—the sweetest, the most delicious I've ever had, maybe by far—and offering at least one to every single person who asked, and for free.

(July 30)

80. "To Respect Each Other's Madness and Right to Be Wrong"

I AM REREADING Susan Sontag's elegy for the writer Paul Goodman in her book *Under the Sign of Saturn*. Goodman was the author, among many other books, of *Growing Up Absurd*, which I pilfered, the paperback, from Gerald Stern's house, and which is in that growing pile of books I plan on reading but have yet to read. It's an unusual elegy because right off the bat Sontag reports that the first few times she met Goodman, when she was a young upstart public intellectual, he was kind of a dick, and seemed disinclined to take Sontag, or maybe any young woman (she suspected), very seriously. Because Sontag can be pretty good at thinking about her thinking—exotic these days; thinking, yes, but scrutinizing one's own thinking especially—she does not automatically believe her assessment. She shakes it some, turns it upside down then right side up again, shakes it a little more—it's a snow globe, you get it—and after the snow settles she says, *Yeah, he could be kind of a dick*. (Also: it's a little more complicated than this. Read the essay.)

Then Sontag explains what she admired about Goodman, whom she considered the most important American writer of his time. She loves his enthusiasm, his intellectual pugilism, and that he was openly bisexual back in the 1950s. She loves that in addition to sociology, psychology, pedagogy, novels, and essays, he wrote poems, sort of old-timey from the sound of it, which Sontag seems to think of as the highest art (a revelation to me). She loves some of his books more than others, and that his writing could sometimes be awkward, which I think she says twice. She loves that he's a polymath, an amateur, an autodidact, and though it's not how they said it back then, she loves that he didn't stay in his lane, despite taking some lumps on account of it. It is obvious that he is a model for her, although she didn't like everything about him, which strikes me not only as descriptive, but as rhetorical. The argument being that, although we are, most of us, sometimes dicks—by which I mean unkind, bumbling, nasty, stupid, violent, profoundly wrong, or, simply, probably, not the truest expression of ourselves—there's also probably stuff about us to love. Most adults know this, whether we let on or not.

I remember one time, because I was not yet an adult, and not knowing I wasn't, as a way of writing someone off—as is so often the case, I was joining a bandwagon; as is so often the case, the writing off was justifying an action I felt ambivalent about—I declared to my friend that the person to be written off was a liar. (Oh: writing off is one of the sadder literary endeavors, don't you think?) I said *Man fuck that liar*, as though I was brushing the crumbs from my hands. My friend, a sometimes sage, said something along the lines of, *Just because someone's a liar you don't have to write them off. You just don't believe everything they say*. It knocked my little baby head all the way off my full-grown shoulders, not only because it alerted me to the fact that I was quick and easy with the writing off, but because I think my friend was implying something along the lines of *that's just how he's broken*, which I've taken, over the years, to mean *you're probably broken in some ways too.*

The refutation, or the refusal, or the *hiding* of which is like fuel to the carceral ember in us, which seems, some days these days, more on fire than ever. It seems, some days these days, like we're a bunch of cops hunting for who's messed up—(trigger warning: *all of us*)—which mess-ups, some days these days more than ever it seems, can be terminal. As though the worst of what we've been is the whole of who we are. You know how they said it in the old-timey movies when they knew they were caught, about to be hauled in or driven over the cliff: *We're finished.* Which, being creatures, we never are; we change until we die, and even then, depending on where you go, you might become soil and worm scat and nutrients to be sucked into the flower whose nectar becomes honey.

But the real sorrow and loss, and what I think of as the danger, is the persistent inquisitional threat and fear of being finished, or *finished off,* not only on account of having actually messed up—you know, a real egregious fuck-up—but of having been *incorrect*, which sometimes means little more than not agreeing or following suit or doing as we're told or staying in our lanes. Being wrong some days these days simply means having a different take, it means *thinking different*, for which you'd think with all the diversity committees everywhere we'd have some tolerance, or curiosity, or even taste.[1]

Anyway, probably it's clear but if not let me make it so: this elegy for Goodman is so moving to me, it's a

1 Worth noting: Michael Pollan once observed that as cooking shows proliferated, people cooked less.

model for me, because, first, Sontag doesn't condemn or convict Goodman. She does not write him off. She describes him. She *regards* him. Complicatedly, unhagiographically, which to me, yes, is evidence of a kind of maturity, but it's also an expression of love, and suggests we, too—bumbling, flailing, hurting, failing, changing—deserve to be regarded, and we deserve to be loved.

But second, and just as important these days, when being *liked* sometimes seems the first and last objective, when being on the team and in agreement and going along and such sometimes seems the goal, when being "good" is the bottom line—or rather, being *perceived* as such is—this elegy reminds me how indispensable are those writers and artists and public intellectuals who are otherwise concerned. Who are more committed to their work, to the questions animating their work, than they are to being likeable. Who are not primarily interested in our approval, and whose work is not meant to affirm us. Who refuse the mandates of what they should think, or how. Of what they should make, and when. Exceedingly precious these days, endangered even, these wingnuts and weirdos. Who don't fit or go along. Who are more committed maybe to *the good* than to being "good." Who are more interested in truth than laurels maybe. Who are more wedded to beauty maybe than fame. Or maybe who just reside on another planet, who knows.

Regardless of why they do it (or don't, as is often the case), without them we're like a bunch of goddamned dalmatians. Or better yet, by which I really mean worse yet, much worse yet, we're like that one kind of potato they were growing when the blight hit in Ireland. Actually, and worse yet still, much worse: we're the people who starved.

(July 31)

81. My Birthday, Again

HERE WE ARE again—despite being an incompletist, I've completed another year of delights. Or maybe I should say another year of delights has completed me. I slept in after a long drive to my mom's from Memphis, woke up around eleven thirty to find Stephanie and my mother sitting in her living room, with the TV muted, chatting away. They both did some happy birthdaying, and I rolled around in it like a pig in shit, hamming it up, asking them to do things for me, all the while with the firm conviction that if anyone is to be celebrated today, it's really my dear mother, who did a lot of the work, and who ought to kick her feet up, but I'm keeping that to myself. I looked at my phone and there was a nice little pile of notes, little missives of gladness and blessed-day-ness, to each of which I noticed, by the third or fourth reply, that if you're lucky, on your birthday you get to say thank you over and over. Seems reasonable to me.

After about four hours of visiting—all of us still in our PJs, I hadn't even put on a shirt yet—we got dressed and went to my favorite café in Harrisburg, which I thought was open until four, but in fact, we realized after we parked and walked up to the door, closed at three. No problem, it was a nice drive, and we headed over to the Goodwill Bins, which means pre-sorted Goodwill, piles of undifferentiated stuff in bins, a place my brother loves to go, and maybe a little bit I was invoking him, since he's down in Florida. I found a beautiful white linen shirt that doesn't fit me, a book of Alice Munro stories, and a Japanese stoneware mug, perfect in every single way, all of which ran Stephanie a buck or two.

We went home, I had some more thank-yous on my phone, and as I always do on my birthday, I got into a nice, long workout that, the older I get, the more loving I make. As much stretching as burpees. As much mobilizing as jumping lunges. Then we gussied up to eat at the Indian joint, which we realized, walking in, was ten minutes from closing. But no problem, they were kind enough to make our food to go. The kid taking our order apologized twenty times because the website is old, but we were glad, we tried to convince her, more thank-yous, etc.

When we got back home and dished up, taking care to warn my mother about what was a little spicy, my mom put on "Y.M.C.A." by the Village People, one of her favorite songs. (Delight: That one of my mom's favorite songs is "Y.M.C.A.," by the Village People. And double delight that she loves how the blue hairs [as she calls them] at Curves would dance to it between stations, probably not knowing how gay the song was.) Actually, Alexa put the song on, in between recording our conversations. My mom bounced to her seat, danced really, smiling and throwing little half punches in synch with her head tilting this way and that, which is kind of her father's dance, my grandpa's. That's three generations. After that we went on a Bee Gees run, and each time a new song came on my mother would pause her eating—she loved the pakoras, she could take or leave the chana masala, I could tell—and listen very hard by staring at me, almost as though I was her memory, I was her record cabinet, her history—and then when she found it, she'd close her eyes in a kind of bliss before shuddering into her little boxer dance, fork in hand, which we all were doing, dancing to the Bee Gees at the dinner table, eating take-out Indian, which makes it already the best of all days. When Alexa, who I kept calling Siri, fell offline, and hopefully will stay there forever, I took over for her by singing that Methodist hit "How Great Thou Art" in modern classical style, belting it, and though I was not looking at my mother, I could feel her looking at me, sort of impressed—she said quietly, *Oh, they would've loved that at the church in Verndale*—which, in a certain, oblique way, I guess I am sometimes trying to make my mom feel about me, for better or worse. Or to put a finer point on it, as Stephanie noted while my mom was taking the trash out, about some stupid joke or other I made, *You really like to make your mom smile.* And then I did Al Green, who I can sometimes channel (minus his top three or four notes), which my mother reminded me I did on Christian Street, in Philadelphia, after a graduation dinner at Sabrina's, which made my nana not only *lordhammercy*, but shake her ample ass with her index finger in the air. Thank you, Al Green, for bringing Nana to the party.

Time kept flying and we were all pooped from doing jackshit all day, so we started getting ready for bed. My mom was lingering, tidying up, wiping down the counter, tossing some junk mail in the recycling. I gave her a big hug and a kiss, told her thanks for birthing me, sorry for when I was a pain in the ass. She kissed me back and said, *Yeah, I really came through, didn't I.* I laughed and said, *I think I'm the one who came through.* Looking up at me and holding me by the waist, she kind of giggled before saying, *You know, I guess we both did.*

(Aug. 1)

Acknowledgments

YOU MIGHT BE surprised to learn that someone had to tell me—I can't quite recall who, or where, but thank you whoever you are—that delights were sort of like gratitudes, or thank-yous, each one (today I can see Gizmo the cat balanced on a fence stretching his body almost into an S; I can hear a woodpecker banging his face into a tree as accompaniment to the polyphonic choir of birds; the arugula has naturalized and is spreading out in the garden, crawling into the dandelions; my neighbors walked by and one of them told me her weird dream; the sun is out and feeding the world) a kind of bell reminding us of something for which we're probably grateful. Which is to say, it took me long enough to get here, I know, but here we are: *The Book of (More) Delights* might just as well be called *The Book of (More) Thank-Yous*. More and more and more and more.

The first of those thank-yous goes to the many, many people (more than I can remember, I know, I'm sorry!) who so kindly listened to or read or asked questions about or truly helped me understand what I didn't quite know I was getting at or actually pointed me to the words and were like *don't you really mean . . .* or *are you trying to say . . .* or simply *received* these essays as they came along, all of which is to say, thank you to all of the people who in some way helped me write these essayettes: PantsO, Poppa, Kayte(y), Alex, Essence, Chrism, Lala, Yalie, Gito, Treecio, Ara, Toialito, Abdel, Rosie, Barney, Saami, Kat, El, Claire, Walton, J, Bonita, JJ, Rhett, Ro, Amy-Jo, Jeffy, Nutdiggy, Cootie, Nandi, Munnz, Joyce, Lotl, Scot-y, Skeety, Leensky, Wally, Meemee, Ol Girl, Jules, KK, Banana, Biggie Momma, Biggie Sis, Padma, Sneezers, and anyone else who, as I write these things, tolerates, endures, and sometimes even seems to enjoy how often in conversation I say, *yeah, I was thinking of that in a delight I'm working on,* or *ooh, hold up, wanna hear a delight about that?* Among whom, too, are all the students I get to share work with, whom I get to study with—crawling in the leaf litter sniffing the soil thanks to Anna Tsing; getting the potlucks back; going over and over the Rukeyser, over and over the Wideman; listening to each other wonder, each other try, each other unknow, each other beautiful like that in the unknowing. How lucky. And, too, the people at readings or other places time to time who sometimes shyly, sometimes boisterously, sometimes like *you might want to know this*, share their delights with me. Every time it makes me glad. It makes me grateful. Which is also to say I am grateful for all the opportunities I've had to talk with people about delight, about joy, about sorrow, about care in the past years: at readings, in class visits, teaching around, etc. That's lucky! (Also, on my way to one such opportunity, I can't let it go, a guy was playing Stevie Wonder's "Overjoyed" on one of those pianos in the airport. C'mon! Thank you!) And of course, of course, thank you to all of the independent bookstores for their generosity and care and regard, for what they do for their communities, for writers, for books, for ideas; and a little extra thank you to my beloved bookstores here in Bloomington: The Book Corner (thank you forever Margaret!) and Morgenstern's. I am so, so grateful to you.

Also, thanks to all the people at Algonquin who have been so supportive over these past several years, who have cared for the work, and looked out for the work, and who have believed in the work, including Betsy Gleick, Michael McKenzie, Brunson Hoole, and Debra Linn and Travis Smith and Katrina Tiktinsky and a whole bunch of other people probably, too. And again (and again), I want to thank my copy editor, Chris Stamey, who kindly and repeatedly alerts me to how much I get really wrong. And I am especially grateful to my editor, Amy Gash, who just kind of gets it, and when she doesn't, she lets me know, and we talk about it. It has been such a gift, a gratitude, working hard with you on these words, trying to get them as true as they can be, and laughing some while we do so.

Thanks as well to my agent, Liza Dawson, for all you do, more than I even know I'm pretty sure. And Vaughan Fielder, thank you for getting me there, and especially thank you for making sure I get back home. I'm so glad we're friends. For the long, dreamy, rambunctious, hotdamn collaboration we've undertaken.

You know, I am also grateful to all the people who write shortish or fragmenty essaypoemthings, whose books and work I really kind of studied in the process of writing the first one of these—Sarah Ruhl and Rivka Galchen and Claudia Rankine and Beth Ann Fennelly and Eduardo Galeano and Maggie Nelson and Jeff Friedman and Rachel Zucker and Toi Derricotte and C. D. Wright and Montaigne, etc. Lots and lots of etc. But I am also and forever and especially grateful (for more reasons than I could ever articulate in one acknowledgments page, or one book, or maybe one life) to our beloved Gerald Stern, who died as I was revising this book. What a gift, what a miracle, to realize the essayette, the brief, daily, meandering meditation, was actually given to you by who loves you, and whom you love, which maybe is always the case, if we pay attention. I'm saying Gerald Stern's *Stealing History* is the mother, kind of the main mother, of this book. These books. Seriously, go read it and you'll know what I mean. There are so many of us who would have no idea how to sing if we hadn't heard your sweet, plaintive, tinny voice, oh beautiful. You've turned into all of us.

And of course, of course, my beloved Stephanie, I mean Steffie-boo, my first and last reader, who hears these things again and again and again (and again and again) hot off the presses. Which means gnarly and not even close. I mean, it ain't pretty. Goddamn, the patience and enthusiasm and curiosity and support mean so much to me. And the *belief*; I should say that. The belief that there's something there. By which I mean something *here*. I am so grateful to you.

And finally, as always: it never stops being a wonder that people read what I write. It never stops being a wonder and a generosity. That you invite my wondering into yours. So to you Dear Reader, again and again and always: thank you.

An Appendix of Brief Delights

WHEN PEOPLE HUM or moan with delight (delicious blueberries, beautiful move on the court, pleasant physical interaction, a busker with a voice from heaven, etc.); the checkout kid at the co-op with pink hair and a concert shirt showing me a magic trick; the woman in an electric wheelchair towing her pal on roller skates; a friend dropping off a cup of seeds; the courtyard as an architectural feature; small talk with strangers; cold water fountains, and how as kids in school we would walk very far (and sometimes be late for class) in order to get to them; how people talk to their dogs, often about how pretty things are, gardens and such; walking at night (with beloveds especially) in the deep dark; the syrupy ooze from the long beans, and the ants who slurp it; the right font (i.e., Garamond); a soft pillow puffy enough; a window that opens; the cacophonous choir of birds shouting *heads up* to each other and all the littler critters when the cats come out; gold teeth;

the old wives, whose advice by the day I more and more believe; that my buddy Scot was neither hurt nor called a nigger by the drunk white college kid who hurled a cinder block through his windshield while Scot was in the driver's seat; how close delight and relief sometimes are; people who always leave something—keys, phone, sunglasses, a book, sneakers—behind; when the kimchi comes out (in?) right; the redbud tree on Third Street with bloodred leaves lit up by the late-day sun; palimpsestic names (i.e., when people of a certain age still refer to Pete's Pub as Tallulah's or Biggie's or Tomorrow's); the word *lookit*; how much the HOPE sign in the neighborhood looks like a NOPE sign; the sophisticated mechanisms of procrastination; gigantic inflatable and probably dangerous-if-a-good-wind-kicks-up holiday decorations; real-life person-to-person recommendations (books, restaurants, views, movies, hikes, dentists, etc.); hugging and exuding gratitude to the brilliant and recently deceased comedian Paul Mooney in a dream; riding a bike hands-free; riding a bike; riding a bike and every once in a while spotting a person driving a car who is not actively using their phone; unannounced visits from friends; people who take a long time to say goodbye; realizing my veggie burgers are probably as good as the veggie burgers I'm always trying to get to in my dreams; a dream in which Wendell Berry is fronting a hard rock band, wearing cargo shorts, tube socks, and high-top Ponys; the volunteer purple Osaka mustard plant glazed with frost; the tether between mercy and gratitude; the beautiful box that holds the magnifying glass for my *Oxford English Dictionary*; how new skateboarders wobble on their boards like toddlers on their feet; boys and their perfume; boys and their very precise sartorial endeavors; the faces people make, and where we stare off into, as we make blind contour drawings; when one of my brilliant undergrads told me they had been browsing the library, an activity I was almost certain had gone extinct (fuck Steve Jobs); that my mother actually says *boy oh boy* and *for Pete's sake*; the taxi driver who suggested Virginia change its name to Land of Trees; how we sometimes don't know the last names of people we really love; dancing a little bit with strangers to good songs in the supermarket; being reminded my batshittery is not unique; walking arm-in-arm; naughty jokes; a wasp poised on my notebook as I was writing as though to adjudicate, periodically buzzing her wings in a way I took to mean applause, to mean *carry on*; the first warm day; drawing cartoons (sometimes naughty) during very important meetings; seeing our beloved, the recently deceased poet Jean Valentine, in the laundromat; seeing actual old people who write on their hands and obviously have not (yet) died of ink poisoning; tables high enough my knees don't hit; how often we wear flying creatures on our clothing; learning some of my childhood friends are doing just fine; the kid working at the vegan bakery finding my notebook and getting it back to me; people in their eighties and nineties walking gleefully; armrests on chairs; couches that foment good dreams (*dream couches*); a tufted titmouse fooling around in some leaf litter at the base of a lilac bush for four, maybe five minutes within arm's reach; how flowers sometimes smell how they look (allium, goumi, honeysuckle); an acquaintance, shirtless, asking me to *spray some of this shit* (sunscreen) *all over my back, would you?*; watching a baby losing his shit (maybe actually) with laughter and catching myself also laughing; the general store; the local bakery (and hardware store and cobbler and typewriter shop and comic book hovel, etc.); the goldfinches who made a nest in my mother's flower basket; deep pockets, socks without holes, and pants that fit right; the return of the potluck; that someone left a roll of many-ply quilted toilet paper in the bathroom at work; mayflies; seeing our beloved, the recently deceased poet Monica Hand, at the New York Botanical Garden; making several unmakeable shots against my friend Abdel in a dream; my mom's strawberry-rhubarb crisp; my friend Ro having a dream in which she was nursing her dog; a pretty scarf; those gold polka-dotted bugs buzzing through the air in coital bliss; when adults in couples dress alike; the way Solange's "Cranes in the Sky" opens like a peony; whoever first decided to plant peonies in the graveyard down the street, which is sort of like a peony farm now; how after hugging people sometimes you smell like them; waking up from dreams with solutions to problems; jaywalking; when someone told me I looked like someone who'd make his own deodorant; cafés without Wi-Fi; my friend Claire staring into the sycamore tree, waiting for the swifts to head out; how we eat without saying so off each other's plates sometimes; bedside and couchside tables made of crates; event posters; noticing how so many of your most comfortable clothes used to belong to your friends; the word *belong*; how clouds and mountains are sometimes indiscernible; morning light through a rectangular window on a wall painted a color probably called tangerine, maybe sunflower; how we sometimes dance, or dance and sing, upon seeing who we love

For Further Reading

I WAS IN conversation in some way with all these books as I wrote this book, and I offer this list as gratitude to the authors who wrote them.

Aguon, Julian, *No Country for Eight-Spot Butterflies: A Lyric Essay*

Alexander, Christopher, et. al., *A Pattern Language: Towns, Buildings, Construction*

Als, Hilton, *My Pinup*

Alsadir, Nuar, *Animal Joy: A Book of Laughter and Resuscitation*

Berman, Marshall, *Modernism in the Streets: A Life and Times in Essays*

Berry, Wendell, *Why I Am Not Going to Buy a Computer*

Boully, Jenny, *The Body: An Essay*

Christle, Heather, *The Crying Book*

Clifton, Lucille, *The Book of Light*

Codjoe, Ama, *Bluest Nude: Poems*

Davis, Lydia, *Essays One*

Delaney, Samuel, *Of Solids and Surds: Notes for Noël Sturgeon, Marilyn Hacker, Josh Lukin, Mia Wolff, Bill Stribling, and Bob White*

Dìaz, Junot, *The Brief Wondrous Life of Oscar Wao*

Dillon, Brian, *Suppose a Sentence*

Du Bois, W. E. B., *Black Reconstruction*

Du Bois, W. E. B., *W. E. B. Du Bois's Data Portraits: Visualizing Black America*

Dyer, Geoff, *See/Saw: Looking at Photographs*

Dyer, Geoff, *The Last Days of Roger Federer: And Other Endings*

Ford, Glen, *The Black Agenda*

Galeano, Eduardo, *Memory of Fire Trilogy*

Galeano, Eduardo, *Open Veins of Latin America: Five Centuries of the Pillage of a Continent*

Galeano, Eduardo, *Soccer in Sun and Shadow*

Galeano, Eduardo, *The Book of Embraces*

Goodman, Paul, *Growing Up Absurd*

Gornick, Vivian, *Taking a Long Look: Essays on Culture, Literature, and Feminism in Our Time*

Graeber, David, *Bullshit Jobs: A Theory*

Guriel, Jason, *On Browsing (Field Notes, 5)*

Hunt, Samantha, *The Unwritten Book: An Investigation*

Hyde, Lewis, *The Gift*

Kimberley, Margaret, *Prejudential: Black America and the Presidents*

Kimmerer, Robin Wall, *Braiding Sweetgrass: Indigenous Wisdom, Scientific Knowledge*

Malcolm, Janet, *Two Lives: Gertrude and Alice*

McKittrick, Katherine, *Dear Science and Other Stories*

Miller, Andrew, *On Not Being Someone Else: Tales of Our Unled Lives*

Morrison, Toni, *The Origin of Others*

Nezhukumatathil, Aimee, *World of Wonders: In Praise of Fireflies, Whale Sharks, and other Astonishments*

Ostriker, Alicia Suskin, *Green Age*

Pinckney, Darryl, *Come Back in September: A Literary Education on West Sixty-Seventh Street, Manhattan*

Reed, Adolph L., Jr., *The South: Jim Crow and Its Afterlives*

Rosal, Patrick, *The Last Thing: New & Selected Poems*

Rudick, Nicole, *What Is Now Known Was Once Only Imagined: An (Auto)biography of Niki de Saint Phalle*

Rukeyser, Muriel, *The Book of the Dead*

Shields, David, *How Literature Saved My Life*

Shields, David, *The Very Last Interview*

Sloan, Aisha Sabatini, *Borealis*

Solnit, Rebecca, *A Field Guide to Getting Lost*

Solnit, Rebecca, *Orwell's Roses*

Solnit, Rebecca, *Recollections of My Nonexistence*

Sontag, Susan, *Under the Sign of Saturn: Essays*

Stern, Gerald, *Death Watch: A View from the Tenth Decade*

Tsing, Anna, *The Mushroom at the End of the World*

White, Simone, *or, on being the other woman*

Wright, C. D., *Cooling Time: An American Poetry Vigil*

Wurman, Richard Saul, ed., *What Will Be Always Has Been: The Words of Louis I. Kahn*

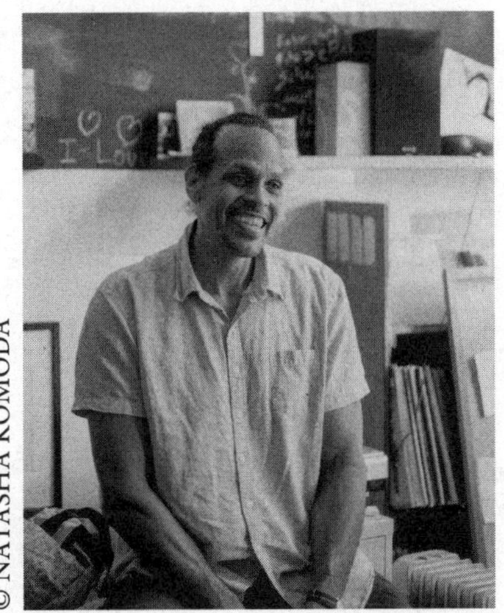

Ross Gay is the author of the essay collections *The Book of Delights*, *Inciting Joy*, and *The Book of (More) Delights*, as well as four books of poetry. The recipient of numerous writing awards, he lives and gardens in Bloomington, Indiana, where he also teaches at Indiana University. His website is rossgay.net.